D0868697

Daniel and Revelation

MADE PLAIN

CHAPTER BY CHAPTER COMMENTARY

By Mark Cambron, M.A., D.D.

WRITTEN FOR EVERYDAY, PLAIN PEOPLE TO UNDERSTAND

Published By

THE SEASIDE PRESS

P. O. Box 146
North Miami Beach, Fla. 33160

Fourth Printing — October, 1972
Fifth Printing — February, 1973

Printed In U.S.A.
By Rapture Press, Inc.
1055 North 21 Avenue
Hollywood, Florida 33020

DEDICATED

To Mary

Without whom my life, my
preaching, and my writings
would be incomplete.

Foreword

It gives me a great deal of pleasure to recommend this marvelous exposition, "Daniel and Revelation Made Plain" written by my good friend, Dr. Mark G. Cambron.

Brother Cambron wrote this book at my suggestion. I consider it one of the finest expositions on Daniel and Revelation that I have ever read. Many of God's people seem to shy away from the prophecies of Daniel and Revelation because they feel that they are too hard to understand. Hence, there is a great need for a book such as this.

Daniel and Revelation must be studied together if one is to understand all the great prophecies of the end time. Daniel explains the book of Revelation and Revelation explains the book of Daniel. They are really supplemental one to the other.

Many godly writers have searched out the precious pearls of prophecy in the two books and have given us marvelous expositions, but I have never read any book on Daniel and Revelation which has impressed me more than this one.

I am sure that each reader will find this book remarkably interesting. Dr. Cambron has a way of making Bible truths so simple and easy to understand. Good books ought to be interesting, and this one certainly is.

Any Christian who will take time to read and study this fine commentary on Daniel and Revelation will surely be blessed. It is both a privilege and a pleasure to commend this book to the Lord's people everywhere.

Charles Halff, Director
The Christian Jew Hour

The Book of Daniel
Introduction

Daniel is a Book which is the object of the Modernists' and unbelievers' attacks. They claim that Daniel could not have been a prophet, because the prophecies are too minute in detail to have been foretold by any man. Therefore, they call him a historian. True, no man could have made such predictions by himself, but a man as an instrument of the Holy Ghost could! The Lord Jesus ended this argument for all time, we believe, by using the words "spoken of Daniel the prophet" (Matthew 24:15).

This great Book has two natural divisions. Chapters 1 through 6 are historical, while Chapters 7 through 12 are prophetical. As this is indeed a Book of prophecy, we believe and shall endeavor to show that even the first six chapters can be applied to future events during the coming Tribulation.

Of all the Old Testament prophets, we know more of the man Daniel. He was of noble, if not royal, blood. He was carried away into the Babylonian captivity in 606 B.C., at about the age of twenty years, and there he remained during the entire seventy years (Jeremiah 25:11).

Should one study this Book from the original languages, he would find that It is written in two languages. Chapters 1 through 2:3 and Chapters 8 through 12 are in Hebrew. Chapters 2:4 through 7:28 are in Aramaic, the ancient language of Syria, which is substantially identical with Chaldean, the ancient language of Babylonia. Thus it can be seen that those things which are spoken concerning the Jews are written in Hebrew, while the things spoken pertaining to the Gentiles are written in their languages.

Daniel is one of the few spotless characters in the Scriptures. Not even a hint of sin is charged against him. He is not mentioned by name in the great "faith" Chapter of Hebrews 11; yet, we believe he is referred to as the one who "stopped the mouths of lions" (Hebrews 11:33).

The prophecy of Daniel covers the "time of the Gentiles" from Nebuchadnezzar to the Antichrist, or is better defined as the "time when Israel is without her king."

The Book of Daniel
Chapter I

I. *The Prophet* (Read verses 1-7).

Someone may point out immediately that Daniel's account differs with Jeremiah's account concerning the besieging of Jerusalem. Daniel places it in the third year, while Jeremiah puts it in the fourth year. They are both right, of course. Daniel states the beginning of the siege, while Jeremiah declares its consummation.

Daniel, along with his Hebrew companions, was taken away to Babylon during the first deportation. The second one occurred eleven years later. Naturally, a question arises, "Why were these noble young men spared?" To begin with, we learn that the king spared those who were full of wisdom, those whom he might instruct in the things of the Babylonians, and those whom he would later appoint to some governmental office. In many countries, from Daniel's day until the last two decades, the only persons allowed to pursue their education were the priests and the nobility. Education was for the classes rather than for the masses. Hence, these four young Hebrew men were already "educated" and were chosen to continue their study; however, this was to be only under the guidance of the Babylonian court. Yet, to keep them from revolting or urging their seed to rebel in the future, they were rendered eunuchs (Isaiah 39:5-7).

Their provisions were the best; they were guaranteed to be the same as the king's. Truly, much was expected of them in the future, when they were to receive their high appointment.

They were citizens of Babylon now and were to live as Babylonians. They were to think and worship as Babylonians. They were even given Babylonian names; Daniel (whose name means "God is my Judge") was changed to Belteshazzar, meaning "Whom Baal Favors"; Hananiah (whose name means "Beloved of the Lord") was changed to Shadrach, meaning "Illumined By The Sun God"; Mishael (whose name means "Who Is As God") was changed to Meshach, meaning "Who Is Like Venus"; and Azariah (whose name means

"The Lord Is My Help") was changed to Abednego, meaning "The Servant of Nego."

II. *The Problem and the Purpose* (Read verses 8-10).

Here were young Hebrew men who were spiritual not only by birth but by choice. By the word **spiritual** we mean the carrying out of the Law of God in the strictest manner. They were now located far from the land of promise; the house of worship (Solomon's temple) was now in ashes. The people of God were dispersed; the priests were disrobed of their sacred office — thus, no sacrifices and no atonement. In view of all this, were they set free from all obligations to God, free to live as the ungodly? Nebuchadnezzar was their king, their captor, and his wishes were to be obeyed. Should all restraint be thrown overboard? Should they live with abandoned freedom the same life as those without God? No, for their God was not just the God of Palestine, but He was the God of all gods; He was the God even in and over Babylon, and their obligation to Him did not cease because of a geographical change or a difference in society.

Daniel vowed in his heart that the standard would not be lowered, that obedience to his God demanded the same life of separation whether he lived in Babylon or whether he could remain in Israel. He knew that strong drink would not strengthen him in his worship; he would not lower himself to eat the meat of the king — swine's flesh. His life was still to be Kosher; his food was still to be Kosher — clean! God was to dominate him completely.

III. *The Proposition* (Read verses 11-14).

God will always provide "helps" along the way for those who will not compromise in their service for Him. Daniel and his companions fell into favor with the prince of the eunuchs and begged him to let them prove by their clean eating that God's dietary laws were superior to those of the court. Only ten days were requested. God's ways need only a short time to prove their worth. To try to do what God suggests demands only faith in HIM! His ways are the best ways. The men of faith have proved it.

IV. *The Profit* (Read verses 15-21).

Proof positive was the result! Daniel and his men were the healthiest of the lot. They ate pulse (plain vegetables) which proved its worth; it also proved the wisdom of God. He knows what is best for man for He made man, and He created food for man. How wonderful it is to trust Him for the very necessities of life. He knows what is best, for He is God!

Their wisdom increased and surpassed the wisdom of the others tenfold. Daniel practiced his faith, not in order to become better than his associates, but to please his Lord.

V. *The Prospect*

It is true that Chapter 1 is in the historical division of this great Book, but by **application** we can see its worth prophetically. During the coming Tribulation, when Israel will be again scattered throughout the Gentile world, there will be a much larger number who shall separate themselves unto the service of their Lord — yes, 144,000 of them. "These are they which were not defiled with women; for they are virgins" (Revelation 14:4) — 144,000 eunuchs! These shall be they whom the Lord Jesus described as "eunuchs which have made themselves eunuchs for the kingdom of heaven's sake" (Matthew 19:12). These are the preachers who shall spread the Gospel of the Kingdom during the Tribulation. They, too, shall not marry nor bear seed, but shall live wholly and holily unto their Lord. Like Daniel, they shall be rewarded for their devotion to God.

The Book of Daniel
Chapter II

I. *Revelations of God* (Read verse 1).

"God who at sundry times and in divers manners spake in time past unto the fathers by the prophets" (Hebrews 1:1). This statement of God clearly declares that there were several means by which God revealed His Word unto men. **Dreams** were one of these methods. This great chapter portrays the fact that God revealed His Word in a dream, and in the dream of an unregenerated monarch at that.

There is a difference between a dream and a vision. A **dream** has been described as that which is seen by the dreamer just before waking consciousness and sound sleep and before sound sleep and waking consciousness. A **vision** is what its name implies — that which can be seen (not in a dream) with the eyes closed while the beholder is fully conscious. God did reveal His Word to His prophets in the Old Testament by visions as well as in dreams.

As this dream is unfolded and the interpretation given, we cannot help but see clearly that it is not the person who gives us the Word, but God. People are mere instruments — "for we have this treasure in earthen vessels, that the excellency of the power may be of God, and not of us" (2 Corinthians 4:7).

II. *Requirement by the King* (Read verses 2-13).

Nebuchadnezzar awoke with a start; he was fearful because of a dream, and though he was deeply troubled, he could not remember what he had dreamed. We can see the plight of this great world ruler. He knew that the very truth of the dream meant something drastic, either for him or for those surrounding him. Being an unregenerated man, without the Holy Spirit, he could not have known the meaning of the most simple things of life about him. He, like many before him and like millions after him, resorted to the inventions of any and all men who could even hint as to what the future held. Surrounded by his advisors (magicians, astrologers, sorcerers, and Chaldeans), he called upon them to tell him not only the interpretation of the dream, but the very dream itself. First, there were the **Magicians** (fortune tellers, etc., those who used magic to tell the future); and then there were the **Astrologers** (those who believed that they could foretell future events by the stars, that these heavenly bodies guided the destinies of mankind); also, the **Sorcerers** (those who used witchcraft, who became tools of Satan to unveil the unknown); and last of all were the **Chaldeans** (a group of men who followed the sciences and proved things by logic, test, and practice). Daniel was considered to be a Chaldean.

All of these men were commanded to give the interpretation and the dream itself! These men appealed to the senses of the king by stating that if he would only tell the dream they would, in turn, give the interpretation. It seemed as though they thought that their ruler was jesting, but he pushed this thought aside when he declared that if the dream and the interpretation were not forthcoming, they were to be liquidated and their homes made a dunghill. How wise this Gentile was. If his counsellors could not tell the past, how could they foretell the future? He emphasized his orders by demanding immediate answers upon pain of death.

Daniel and the three other stalwart Hebrews came under this condemnation.

III. Request by the Prophet (Read verses 14-18).

The need for their God became evident in the lives of this great man and his companions. Perfect resignation was theirs. They were in a foreign country; they had been elevated by this sovereign; and now their lives were threatened by a demand which no other known king had ever made. They must describe a dream which the dreamer himself had forgotten!

It is wonderful for a man to know that **his** God knows **all** things. Truly, Elohim **(the Putter-Forth-of-Power)**, not only holds the world in His hands, but He knows the end from the beginning. **He even knows what could have happened if things had happened that didn't happen.** Surely, He who made man and man's mind, could recall what was put in it, especially when God put it there!

They pled for an extension of time, and it was granted. A prayer meeting was called — an all-night prayer meeting. Daniel and his fellow-believers sought the Lord's wisdom and found it!

IV. *Results of Their Faith* (Read verses 15-45).

Daniel and his men praised their Lord and called for an audience before the king. The judgment of death was stayed, and the dream was recalled.

Not only did God give them the dream, but also the circumstances surrounding it. Just before falling asleep Nebuchadnezzar began to think of himself, of his world-wide kingdom, of death (those things which should come hereafter). Could there be anyone to follow him, to sit upon his throne? Could it be possible for him to **die?** Then God gave him the dream in his sleep and later enabled His prophet to interpret it. There is no God like our God!

This dream of Nebuchadnezzar's describes in detail the entire **Time of the Gentiles** (when Israel is without her king; when the nation of Israel is under Gentile domination). Israel today differs very little from the Israel which existed at the time of Jesus Christ. She still does not possess the old City of Jerusalem. The **time of the Gentiles** still prevails.

The dream consisted of a great image. Its head was of **Gold;** its arms and breast were of **Silver;** its belly was of **Brass;** its legs were of **Iron;** and its toes were of **Iron** and **Clay.** This image existed until a **STONE** cut out without hands smote it and destroyed it. The **STONE** then grew. A stone growing? This denotes the supernatural. It became a great **MOUNTAIN** and filled the earth.

The interpretation revealed that four great kingdoms were to rule the earth: The Head of Gold (Nebuchadnezzar and Babylon); the Arms and Breast of Silver (the coming kingdom of Media and Persia); the Belly of Brass (Greece); and Two Legs of Iron (Rome). Who hasn't read of the "Iron Legions" of Rome? Rome (two legs) had two capitals — the East at Constantinople and the West at Rome. Then there are the Ten Toes of Iron and Clay. These toes contain the same mineral as the Legs, plus an additional ingredient, clay.

Right here we would like to point out to the Bible student the fact that the Church and its age were never known in the Scriptures of the Old Testament (Ephesians 3:1-10). The Old Testament prophets saw the **first** coming of Christ as one mountain peak in the distance and the **second** coming of Christ as another mountain peak, but they did not see the valley in between. That valley in between is the church and its age. Hence, we see Christ's first coming during the Kingdom of Iron (Rome); then at His death, burial and resurrection, with the descent of the Holy Spirit, a gap (known as the Church age) separates the iron legs from the iron and clay toes. Consequently, when the gap closes (the end of the Church age), the kingdom of Iron will be revived (Rome), and mingled with it shall be clay, which is described by Daniel as the "seed of men"—the rule of the people! In our own day we are seeing the rule of the people taking over — in government, in business, in law, and in ecclesiastical circles. Some of these movements have arisen in our own day, such as facism, nazism, and communism. All are the rule of the people, but they are under different names.

Verses 44 and 45 state clearly that in the days of the ten kings (described as the **Ten Toes**) the great **STONE** which grows into a Mountain destroys the entire image. That STONE is **Christ!** When He comes the Second Time He will truly put under foot all the ungodly rule of the earth and put to an end the Time of the Gentiles. The **Mountain,** of course, is Christ's kingdom, which shall cover the whole earth.

As we view this image we cannot help but notice the lessening of the worth of the metals — gold down to iron and clay. At the same time we are aware of the increasing strength of the metals — gold up to iron (though clay may be present, the strength of the iron is there).

As the gold kingdom (Babylon) is taken over by the silver domain (Media and Persia), the Silver empire is the composite of the two. It is the same as when the Brass kingdom (Greece) conquers the Silver empire. The Brass takes in the territory of all three. Then the Iron kingdom (Rome) takes in all the world as it conquers the Brass empire.

From this great prophecy of the Time of the Gentiles portrayed by the image, we are led to believe that there will be only four great world kingdoms. Hence, the Roman Empire shall be revived. From an article in the New York

Times' Sunday magazine section of 1951, the writer (a historian rather than a minister) states that the Roman Empire of the time of the Caesars is revived now in the United Nations, even to the dividing of the Nation of Germany. The Romans could only conquer the Western Division of Germany, and that section is now under the direction of the United Nations — the Revived Roman Empire. Is it really possible for Rome to be revived? Truly, she is much alive today. Our days and months are named for Roman gods and emperors. Our coins bear the print of its gods. Medical and botanical terms are still written in the language of Rome — Latin. The ceremonies of the Catholic Church are chanted in Latin. We may ask, "Why was Italy forgiven all of its war debts of World War II?" Another question arises, "How many countries are there which are not headed by, followers of the Church of Rome?" Therefore, Rome will be ruler of the earth. The Church Age, as stated before, was never known in the Old Testament. Truly, this age, or dispensation of grace, is parenthetical. When the Church is raptured, things will continue as they were before the Church began. Israel will be back in the land as at the time of Christ; the Jewish people will be back under the Mosaic Law, and Rome will again be ruling the world. We must state at this time, although we shall comment more fully as we come to it, that Russia shall be "co-existing" during the first part of the Tribulation along with the Ten-Toed Kingdom. Later revelation (Revelation 17) states that the Ten-Toed Kingdom shall be ruled over by ten kings who shall not receive their power until the middle of the Tribulation, and then they will give their power over to the Antichrist. Consequently, the one-world government is set up **after** Russia is destroyed.

With the second Coming of the Messiah, God's absolute rule is set up, and the glory of the Lord shall cover the earth as waters cover the sea.

V. *Recognition With Honors* (Read verses 46-49).

The king was true to his word. He promoted Daniel and his three brethren and gave glory to the God of Daniel.

The Book of Daniel

Chapter III

In Chapter 2 the king dreamed a dream which consisted of an image with a head of gold, breast and arms of silver, belly of brass, legs of iron, and toes of iron and clay. This image was given by God and interpreted by the prophet of God to foretell the **Times of the Gentiles.** Nebuchadnezzar was told that he and his empire were the Head of Gold. Now in this chapter we see him building an image.

I. *Exalted Pride of the King* (Read verses 1-5).

In the king's dream the head of the image was only of gold. His pride caused him to make an image which was **all** of gold. No doubt the image bore his own likeness, and by the erection of it he tried to unify all religions into one. To worship it would be to worship Nebuchadnezzar also.

We would like to point out the number **6** in this portion of the chapter. The image was **60** (6 x 10) cubits high and **6** cubits wide. The command to fall down and worship the image was to be given by the sounding of the **6** instruments. The number **6** is man's number. He was created on the 6th day; he was to labor 6 days, etc. In Revelation 13:18 we read that the number of the Antichrist is **666** — three sixes. The verse states it is the number of a man.

II. *Execution Promised for Disobedience* (Read verses 6-15).

Those who were haters of God and haters of His believers at once told the king of the insubordination of the three Hebrew men. The king himself made an added appeal to these men to comply to the edict. It was a threat more than an appeal. They were members of his court; he had used them for his own purposes at another time; decency and propriety demanded that he give them another chance to comply.

III. *Escape Possible by God* (Read verses 16-25).

"With God all things are possible" — "Is there anything too hard for the Lord?" To the believing heart, nothing is impossible with his God. He is the God of the impossible.

These men believed this with all their hearts. The **only** thing which would keep God from doing the impossible and cause the fire not to consume them was His **will!** These men already had the victory. They had already turned their lives over to the Lord, saying, "Thy will be done"; this was now the theme of their lives. He who had created fire could easily put it out.

In verses 17 and 18 these men of God clearly state that their God was able and would deliver them from the fire; but if He did not, it would not be that He was unable to deliver them, but rather that He chose to let them burn.

This is a true account of the lives of three men who trusted the Lord. They, like us, did not wish to be cast into the fire, but if that were the will of God they were willing. "And we know that all things work together for good to them that love God, to them who are the called according to his purpose" (Romans 8:28). The purpose of God was to be worked out in the lives of these true believers. The fire became inevitable. How true it is, as one stated, "Whenever you speak to a child of God you know that he is either about to go into the fire, or is coming out of it, or is **in** it." Yes, all of God's children have to have their fire experience. It may be of long duration, or it may be only a short time. God is the only one who determines how long and how hot these fiery trials are to be.

These men never faltered in their faith; neither did the king waver in his determination that they should perish. The fire was heated seven times hotter in order to multiply their suffering. However, if they should be consumed, they would die seven times quicker. The fire became so intense that the men casting them into the furnace were slain. As these men stood, unhurt, in the midst of the furnace, they were accompanied by "the Angel of the Lord." Some have proposed that this angel was no one other than the Lord Jesus Christ, as He is described as **"The Angel of the Lord."** How true He is to His Word when He says, "I will never leave thee nor forsake thee" (Hebrews 13:5). Then there are others who point to the true translation, "**an** angel of the Lord." And this, too, substantiates the Word when It says, "Are they not all ministering spirits, sent forth to minister for them who shall be the heirs of salvation?" (Hebrews 1:14). There was an extra person with them in the midst of the fire; God Himself will provide a heavenly companion for you as you walk in your furnace of fire: Christ, Himself!

IV. *Examination Proved the Power* (Read verses 26-30).

This whole experience was brought to its climactic height when the king commanded them to come forth, and they did come forth, walking. They had been bound and then cast into the furnace, but now they were loosed by the power of the flames which had been lighted for their destruction. No power of hurt was found upon them; no clothes were singed; there was no smell of smoke. In fact, they were cleansed by their ordeal. How true it is today, that when the child of God comes out of his adversity, he is enriched by the experience; his faith is increased, and his testimony is to the praise of the Lord. Yes, the child of God is like silver that is tried seven times—the dross is gone, and a purity exists. Of course, we are not talking about the taking away of sins nor of the so-called eradication of the sinful nature, but merely of the purifying process which God has ordained for all His children.

To those of you who are walking in the flames, hear the encouraging words of Isaiah 43:2b — "When thou walkest through the fire, thou shalt not be burned; neither shall the flame kindle upon thee." What a promise! And then more balm of encouragement is anointed to the troubled heart with these words of I Peter 5:10, "But the God of all grace, who hath called us unto his eternal glory by Christ Jesus, **after that ye have suffered a while,** make you perfect, stablish, strengthen, settle you." God knows when it shall be enough. Then He will stop it.

Some are anxious to know what became of Daniel at this time. We must concur with this and believe that Daniel must have been in other parts of the empire when the edict to worship the image was given. We are led to believe by other accounts of his life that had he been present, he too would have defied the injunction and would have taken his stand with his Hebrew brethren.

Because of the faith of these three men, Nebuchadnezzar was led to recognize the power of Elohim, the "putter-forth-of-power," and he demanded death of those who spoke disparagingly of the God of Israel.

The testing is always before the blessing. Abraham had similar testings and then the blessings; Jacob was surely tried, but after the trials came the blessings. Now, the blessings were theirs — promoted by him who had first tried to destroy them. The hand of God is seen in it all. He holds His children in His hands, and nothing can come into their lives but what He wills. Let us all join these three men of faith and say, "Thy will be done."

By application we can see a prophetic meaning in this image and the command to worship it. In the 17th chapter of Revelation we see that a great image of the Antichrist will be erected with the compelling demand that the world worship it. Praise God for those who shall be beheaded for not worshipping the image nor taking the mark of the beast in their foreheads or in the palm of their hands during the Tribulation. God shall elevate them by raising them from the dead and giving them the privilege to rule and reign with Christ for 1,000 years.

Now for a drastic contrast between these three Hebrew believers and the Lord Jesus, the Messiah!

1. They had their furnace of fire.
2. They were placed there because they would not sin.
3. They were attended by one like a Son of God.
4. They were comforted.
5. They were remembered by God.
6. They came out alive.
7. They came out of the furnace and later died, awaiting the Resurrection.

1. He endured the fires of the wrath of God when He tasted death for all men.
2. He was placed there on the cross because of our sins.
3. He, the Son of God, was aided by no one.
4. He was not comforted.
5. He was forsaken by God.
6. He died.
7. He came out of the grave to become the Resurrection and the Life.

The Book of Daniel

Chapter IV

This chapter begins with the testimony of King Nebuchadnezzar concerning his terrible ordeal and the things he had to experience before he was willing to submit to the God of Israel, the God of all gods, the one and only true God! He verifies the teaching of other portions of the Scriptures that the **Kingdom of God** is everlasting, eternal. God is its King, and the **Kingdom of God** exists, as far as man is concerned, with the beginning of man. Later revelations by the Lord Jesus (John 3) tell us that one must be born again to enter into the **Kingdom of God**. The Kingdom of God differs from the Kingdom of Heaven, as declared only in Matthew's Gospel. The Kingdom of the Heaven(s) is the literal Kingdom of the Messiah here upon earth after the Tribulation. Romans 14:17 describes the **Kingdom of God** as being not meat and drink, but righteousness, peace, and joy in the Holy Ghost. In other words, it is spiritual and moral in its sphere.

As far as man is concerned the Kingdom of God has existed since man has been here. The Old Testament saints were born-again believers, for they were saved; therefore, they entered the Kingdom of God. The Messiah told Nicodemus that he must be born again, and he could have been, although the Messiah had not as yet gone to the Cross.

I. *The Dream Fully Remembered* (Read verses 1-5).

Years before King Nebuchadnezzar had had a dream, but he had forgotten it; now he remembered his new dream, but he was as perplexed as ever, even fearful of its prospects. He was not angry with himself for not being able to recall the dream as before, but was indeed anxious to find its secret meaning, though he was afraid of its consequence. What a plight to be in! He, the supreme ruler of the entire known world, possessed so little wisdom that he was afraid to interpret his own dream. He knew law and executed it; he exercised his will, and he gave in to desire; but as far as knowing God, His Laws and His Will, Nebuchadnezzar was powerless.

II. *The Advisors Completely Baffled* (Read verses 6, 7).

As before, these unregenerated "wise men" were at a loss to interpret Elohim's (God's) message, given through this unclean vessel, Nebuchadnezzar. This time they knew the dream, but they were still puzzled. True, no one can know the things of God but he who knows God. They could do wonders with some fickle little dreamette, but with the revelation of God they stood in darkness, as their sunless hearts showed.

No threats were made against those who couldn't tell the meaning of the dream, and for that reason we are led to believe that the monarch had some hope that he would eventually know the importance of it.

III. *The Prophet Wholly Composed* (Read verses 8-27).

"But at the last Daniel came in before me" — God and God's man is at last subscribed to. Sad to say, we have found the same unbelief in the lives of truly born-again children of God; they try everything, and when things fail, then they "try" the Lord. "Then they cried unto the LORD in their trouble, and he delivered them out of their distresses" (Psalm 107:6, 13, 19, 28). It is doubtful if we would cry unto the Lord if we were not allowed to get into deep distresses. Should distress be your portion, your God has His ear attuned to your cry; call upon Him and He will lead you out.

Daniel was silent for one hour after he heard the dream. Truly, it was a peculiar one — a tree whose branches spread throughout the world, under which man and beast found lodging from the heat of the sun and found its fruit good for food. The birds even made their nests in the branches. All was good until an order was heard from heaven to cut the tree down, leaving the stump and binding it with a band of iron and brass, letting seven times pass over it. The stump was to be left out in the weather, watered by the dew; its heart was to be changed from a man's heart to the heart of a beast.

It was decreed by the "watchers" of heaven. Verse 17 clearly states that all rulers of nations are placed there by the God of Heaven. By this we know that men like Nero, Napoleon, Stalin, Mussolini, and even demon-possessed persons like Hitler were put at the helm of their governments by God — "that the most High ruleth in the kingdom of men, and giveth it to whomsoever he will, and setteth up over it the basest of men." We leave the wisdom of these choices to God, who indeed is All-wise. Heaven itself governs the **kingdom of men.** Nothing, simply nothing, can happen to a people by a king or ruler, except by the will of God. Somewhere the answer is there. If we do not comprehend it now, we shall know one of these days. God's will is known in heaven and is carried on by the "watcher" (No doubt, His angels).

Daniel hesitated to give the correct interpretation, not because he feared the king, but because he felt sorry for the monarch, who was to experience the torture of the damned.

Nebuchadnezzar was that tree whose branches spread to the ends of the earth, satisfying the world's needs. However, he was to go through a terrible period of testing. He was to be cut off from society — not to die — but to become insane and be driven from the faces of men, despised and forsaken, until he would eat grass like the oxen. His body would be wet with the dew; his hair would grow like eagle feathers, and his nails would be like bird claws. He was to remain in this state until he recognized that God ruled the universe instead of man, and that it was God who had placed Nebuchadnezzar upon the throne.

IV. *The King Totally Agrees* (Read verses 28-37).

He did not rage. Was this a simple resignation to the will of God? It was a simple willingness to wait and see if this interpretation were true.

"All this came upon the king, Nebuchadnezzar." What God has promised, He is able also to perform, whether it be a promise of blessing or one of judgment.

In this Scriptural passage we learn that judgment may be postponed, but it cannot be averted. Judgment will come. "He that soweth to the flesh shall reap corruption" is not only for the unbeliever, but it is for the believer as well. "Whatsoever a man soweth, that shall he also reap." And it is so.

One year after Daniel had interpreted the king's dream, Nebuchadnezzar walked in the palace of the kingdom of

Babylon and lifted up his eyes in pride, asking, "Is not this great Babylon, that I have built for the house of the kingdom by the might of **my** power, and for the honor of **my** majesty?" His ego was greatly inflated. This lesson is for all of the rulers of the world, teaching that judgment of like nature will be meted out to them unless they acknowledge that God rules in the kingdom of men. Nebuchadnezzar was driven from men; the heart of a beast was given him, and he lived as an animal for seven years, until he recognized that Elohim of Israel was the God of all gods.

The dream had pictured the stump being saved and bound with a band of brass and iron; the king was spared, and the off-shoots of the stump became greater than ever before. His reasoning returned, along with all of his friends and counselors, and the glory of his kingdom was even greater than before.

The true way up is through humility. It is God who promotes, and He will always lift up those who make themselves low. Yea, God exalts the humble.

The words of this great king leads us to believe that he became a true believer in the God of Israel.

The Book of Daniel

Chapter V

Chapter 5 begins with the adult life of Belshazzar, the king. A number of years have elapsed since the rule of Nebuchadnezzar. Belshazzar was not the son of Nebuchadnezzar as many have proposed; he was a grandson.

Nebuchadnezzar died, leaving two children — a son by the name of Evil-merodach, and a daughter. His daughter had married a man by the name of Neriglissar, and unto them was born an imbecile son, whom they named Laborsoarch. The son of Nebuchadnezzar reigned after the death of his father, but he was assassinated by his brother-in-law, Neriglissar. Neriglissar reigned for about four years and then was killed in battle. His son, the imbecile Laborsoarch, then reigned for nine months and later was beaten to death.

In the meantime the daughter was married again; this time she married Nabonidus. He seized the throne and reigned for seventeen years. Belshazzar was born to them. Belshazzar and his father, Nabonidus, reigned concurrently. At the time of this writing the father was out fighting in the South; Belshazzar was supposedly safe behind the walls of Babylon, while the armies of Media were sieging it. Later on we will understand what Belshazzar meant when he promised the position of "third" in the kingdom. His father was first; he was second; and the man fulfilling his desire was to be third.

I. *Defamation of Things Holy* (Read verses 1-4).

These feasts of the ancient kings have been described by others as banquets which lasted for weeks on end. They began with the meat of kings and the drinking of the best vintage of the kingdom, but as the days passed the mere feasts turned into drunken orgies. The sexual practices that were committed defied publication. Rome continued these feasts, and even in the city of Pompei, which was destroyed by a volcano in 79 A.D., ruins have been discovered which point to this truth. You may visit this ruined city and see there a rectangular pool; it is too small to be a swimming

pool, but it is too large to be just a lily pond. It is a vomitsorium — just what the name implies. During these long
feasts, when the diner could eat no more, he would excuse
himself and go to the vomitsorium, where he would stick a
feather down his throat to relieve himself from the distress of
over-eating. Having completed this ordeal, he would go back
to the table for another helping.

Such was the feast of Belshazzar.

Belshazzar, his noblemen, and their companions thought
their safety was secure. Were they not protected by the walls
of Babylon? The city itself was 20 miles long and 20 miles
wide — 400 square miles. It was surrounded by a wall that
was 300 feet high; it was so large that four chariots could
pass each other on top. There was a very deep moat filled
with water. The river Euphrates flowed under the wall at
one end, then through the entire city, and on till it flowed
out under the wall at the other end. The entire bank of the
Euphrates was lined with marble within the city limits. Iron
fences with brass gates lined the river banks as it flowed
through. Thousands of armed men guarded the fences and
gates. One can see why it would seem impossible to overthrow the city.

The city dwellers, too, thought that they could be protected forever. Records of real estate transactions have been
found which were made during the siege. As for food, the
storehouses were filled with grain which could last seven
years, and there were thousands of acres which were under
cultivation at all times. Fresh meat could be supplied for
years to come by the cattle which were raised upon the farms
enclosed within the city's walls.

Lulled by a sense of false security, Belshazzar was drinking the cup of sin to its bitter dregs. He decided to try a
new sport, so he brought out the vessels which had been consecrated to God (Jehovah), which his grandfather, Nebuchadnezzar, had captured years before. Filling them with wine,
they drank toasts to their false gods of gold and silver, brass
and iron, and wood and stone. The first commandment had
been broken, and the name Jehovah had been defiled! Then
the Word of God came to him.

II. *Dilemma of King Belshazzar* (Read verses 5-29).

A man's hand was seen writing on the wall. Belshazzar was not the only one to see it; it was beheld by the entire group. Fear certainly took possession of the king, for he was the object of the judgment of God; he was the one who had commanded his people to profane the things which were holy. No wonder his knees smote one another.

Urgent appeals were made to his advisors to interpret the writings, but not one of them could reveal the meaning of the words written upon the wall. Finally, the king's mother, the daughter of Nebuchadnezzar, came in and advised him to call Daniel, upon whom his grandfather had called several times.

Daniel was called, and as we see this great man of God standing before this monarch, our eyes are filled with tears of admiration, respect and love. Here was one of God's choicest vessels; he was clean and would never defile himself; even the Gentiles recognized that the Spirit of God rested upon him. Daniel was no longer a young man. He was between the ages of 80 and 90 years. How glorious it is that God does not have an age limit. Daniel had never retired from serving God. We, ourselves, are to serve Him **in** season and **out** of season.

The prophet, true to his calling, gave the meaning of the message of God. The interpretation was not an optimistic one, but the king had never expected that it would be; however, it was final. The king had been weighed in the balances and found wanting. He did not measure up to the standard of God for a king, nor did his morals suggest his continuance. God had numbered the kingdom and finished it. Then Daniel was elevated to the third place into the kingdom, and Belshazzar waited for his death. The kingdom had now been turned over to the Medes and Persians — just like God said it would be in the first dream of Nebuchadnezzar. The Arms and Breast of Silver were to take over the kingdom of Gold. The word Peres is the single form of the word Upharsin.

III. *Destruction of the Babylonian Kingdom* (Read verses 30-31).

How could Media-Persia destroy this great city? They did not destroy it; they captured it. While Belshazzar wined and dined, the armies of Media were far north of the city digging a new bed for the Euphrates river. When it was completed the old channel was stopped and closed, leaving the water to find its way into its new bed. Then the army, numbered in the tens of thousands, marched on to the city, even under the walls where the old river bed ran. It was only a matter of time until the iron fences were destroyed, the Babylonian soldiers killed, and the king slain. The populace was spared, for the people of the city continued as before, paying tribute to Media-Persia instead of Babylon.

Daniel was also spared that he might be used in the new government by the new king.

There has been much trouble over this man Darius. Some authorities have stated that there were several Darius', but history does not provide anything of note concerning this man who conquered Babylon. The error of these historians is that they have been looking to the Persian empire for this Darius. He was not a Persian; he was a Median. Look up the history of Media, and you will find this man Darius, who headed the new government, whose capital was now in the same city, Babylon.

It is well to note that in Revelation 9:13 and 16:12 we find that the kings of the land of the rising sun (East) will come by way of the river Euphrates; by some means that river bed will be dry again; this time it will be to allow the passing of the armies of the Antichrist from the East to be united with him for the battle of Armageddon.

The Book of Daniel

Chapter VI

The Kingdom of the Breast and Arms of Silver is now the mistress of the world. She is a twofold nation — two Arms of Silver, joined tightly into one government.

The Silver is stronger, but the deterioration in the worth of the metal is noted. There has been no one as strong in rule as Nebuchadnezzar; what he willed was done. He could make a man and then break him. He was the head of Gold. The strength of the government was increasing, but absolute rule of the sovereign was limited. The king of Media-Persia could make any law he chose, but he could never change it.

I. *Decree* (Read verses 1-9).

Darius set 120 princes over the kingdom, with three presidents over them. Daniel was one of the latter. God-given wisdom was still in this man of God and was recognized by the new sovereign. The recognition of Daniel by the king stirred up the jealousy of his fellow magistrates. They were determined that Daniel should be destroyed and his office given to another.

Most men are human enough to be guided into the making of unfair and unwise decisions when someone appeals to their vanity. These men appealed to Darius' vanity by saying, "O king, live forever." Think of it — his own princes and presidents were so thankful to have him rule over them, that in order to show their appreciation, they wanted him to establish a statute which decreed that no man could make a request of another man nor of a god for 30 days, except of Darius himself; if anyone disobeyed he would be cast into the den of lions.

Without seeking advice, or taking time for consideration, Darius immediately signed the decree. Now they thought they had trapped Daniel. They knew that he loved his God. They knew he cared not for any rule of man which would try to separate him from his God; however, the den of lions held no threat for this man. They knew Daniel. They knew he would choose the den of lions in order to worship and ask petitions of his God; they knew that Daniel was as good as destroyed already.

II. *Defiance* (Read verses 10-11).

This was defiance, pure and simple. He could not plead ignorance of the law, as no one was allowed such a plea. He knew that the edict was signed; he knew that it was law for 30 days. He knew that it was in effect, and he also knew the penalty for non-compliance, but he prayed to his God anyway!

Couldn't he have used a compromise? Couldn't he have waited for just 30 days? All believers in the Lord are told to obey those who have the rule over them. We must obey the higher powers. When should one obey his government and when should he not obey it? We are to obey our government at **all** times, until that government defies the Law of God. Then, with freedom of conscience, we should obey God rather than the government of man. May God preserve our dear land, for it was built upon the Law of God — yes, God bless America! May the United States of America continue in that direction.

Prophecy teaches us that there is to be doom for all world governments, and that there shall be many like Daniel who shall defy the World Ruler (Antichrist); and they, too, shall know what it means to be cast into the destruction proposed by the Dragon and his Beast.

Daniel respected the king, but he had no respect for his God-defying law. So he prayed as he had never prayed before! God bless such men, who will stand up and worship their God.

III. *Defense* (Read verses 12-14).

The enemies of this servant of God were watching for his disobedience, and they found him on his knees, praying to his Lord. God was truly real to his soul, and his habits of serving Him did not change.

The king was then notified of Daniel's insubordination and was urged to comply with his decree. The king realized that it had been a trap. He became displeased with himself and determined to secure Daniel's release, but he had made the law; that had been easy, but he could not change it; the law of the Medes and Persians could not be altered. He was a victim of his own carelessness.

IV. *Defeat* (Read verses 15-23).

Defeat? Of course not! The glee of the princes turned into gloom for Darius, but it brought about the grace of God for Daniel!

Into the den of lions Daniel was cast. Humanly speaking, there was nothing to expect but death. However, Daniel had seen the hand of the Lord in his life before. He had learned of the deliverance of his three companions from the fiery furnace. Could not God deliver again? He could and would!

Dear heart, you, too, may have to be cast (literally or figuratively) into a den of lions for the Messiah's sake. You may be there now; but, remember, **He** is able to deliver thee!

Darius could not eat his dinner that nght, nor would he allow music to be played. Even sleep fled from him. His mind was upon one man who was in a den of lions because of the king's own foolishness in making a foolish decree, by which foolish men had foolishly fooled him.

Early in the morning he ran to the mouth of the den, calling, "Daniel, is thy God able to deliver thee?" A muffled voice came from the sealed den, "O king, live for ever!" Then came praise to the One who had delivered him. An angel had been sent unto Daniel, and the lions' mouths had been closed. Oh, how our imaginations are carried away with this den experience of Daniel. We do not know what went on throughout the night; we only know that Daniel was conscious of the presence of the Lord. How great are these testings we go through. In and through them all we become conscious of the nearness and preciousness of the presence of the Lord Jesus. How great is God!

V. *Destruction* (Read verses 24-28).

Both the Bible and history point to illustrations of the destruction of those who planned by unlawful and vile means to harm the innocent. As a man metes out to others, so it will be meted out to him. The very men who had planned to liquidate Daniel were destroyed, with their families, by the same means that had been formulated for Daniel.

Darius, like Nebuchadnezzar, acknowledged the superiority of the God of Israel. All of his subjects were commanded to respect Him, and the Kingdom of God was truly recognized as that which is eternal!

Thus ends this historical section of the Book of Daniel. While much of these past accounts are historical, yet we see the prophetical applications which can be made to them. Beginning with Chapter 7, however, it is all prophetical, pure and simple.

The Book of Daniel
Chapter VII

Dreams!

At this time God was still using this method to reveal His secrets to men. Remember, He does not have to use this method today, for we now have the full revelation of the sacred Scriptures complete in the Bible.

In the preceding chapters we found that God revealed the future (the part relating to them) to the Gentiles through their dreams. Now the Lord is revealing the future through the dreams of His Jewish prophets for the things concerning Israel in the consummation of their fulfillment.

Even as Daniel was called upon to interpret the dreams of others, he had need for others to reveal the meaning of his dreams.

I. *The World Governments* (Read verses 1-8 and 15-25).

Verses 1-8 describe the beasts, and verses 15-25 interpret them.

In verse 4 the Nation of Babylon is depicted as the Lion. Though verse 17 states that they shall arise out of the earth (which they did), the interpretation does not mean that the nation after Babylon is described as the Lion. Turning back to verse 4 you will notice that the **rise** of the Lion government is not mentioned, but its **end** is. This Lion government corresponds to the Head of Gold empire of Daniel 2.

Verse 5 describes the **Media-Persia** government as the Bear. Very little is spoken about it, either in the statement or in the interpretation. This Bear government corresponds to the Two Arms and Breast of Silver of Chapter 2. It raises itself up on one side (showing that it naturally possesses two sides), the one side rising to prominence first. The two sides were the same as the Two Arms of Silver. The three ribs in the mouth of the Bear denote the three kingdoms it subdued in rising to World power — Babylon, Lydia and Egypt.

Verse 6 reveals that **Greece** is the Leopard with Four

Heads. Someone has said that a better word for Leopard is Panther. Whatever is taken literally does not deny the fact that this beast is Greece. The Leopard, or Panther, empire corresponds with the Belly of Brass in Chapter 2. Please keep in mind the Four Heads of the Leopard, or Panther, empire, for this truly agrees with the Four Horns of the He Goat in Chapter 8.

In verse 7 the **Roman** empire is pictured as a Dreadful and Terrible Beast with Ten Horns. The Ten Horns correspond with the Ten Toes of Chapter 2. Verse 8 goes on to reveal that three of these horns shall be plucked out by a Little Horn, who shall be the ruler during the last days before the Messiah returns. Who can this Little Horn be but the Antichrist? Verses 19-27 describe this Dreadful and Terrible Beast and the Little Horn more fully as to the rule of the government. The Little Horn shall rule the world with absolute authority and subdue everything that gets in his way. He shall blaspheme the most High God (El Elyon). No doubt he shall change the calendar from A.D. (in the year of our Lord) to begin with his birth, or his reign. His rule shall last for three and one-half years. He shall continue until the Ancient of Days shall come, and when the Messiah (Ancient of Days) returns, the rule of the Little Horn shall be broken. We would have you keep in mind the Little Horn of Chapter 8. We believe that the Little Horn of Chapter 7 is the same person as the Little Horn of Chapter 8.

II. *The Wonderful God* (Read verses 9-14 and 26-28).

There is only **one** Person called Wonderful in the Scriptures, and He is the Messiah! — "and his name shall be called Wonderful, Counsellor, The Mighty God, The Everlasting Father, the Prince of Peace" (Isaiah 9:16). And He is truly the Lord Jesus, the Messiah.

Just look at His description in verses 9-10. We see Him described in like manner in Revelation, Chapter 1. Then the Messiah is described as the Son of Man. Certainly this reveals the two natures of the Messiah. He is God (the Ancient of Days), and He is Man (the Son of Man). The two natures blend to be the one Person, the Messiah. This can be seen in a somewhat similar account as found in Revelation 5. The Messiah is described to be God on the throne, with a scroll in His hands; and again He is portrayed as a Lamb, as though it had been recently slain. The Messiah is both — His divine nature revealed as He sits **upon** the throne — His human nature unveiled as He stands **before** the throne. The two compose the one Person, the Messiah!

The "Son of Man" is the **Millennial Title** of the Messiah (Psalm 8:4-9), and it is when He comes as the Son of Man that the yoke of the Little Horn is broken and the Kingdom of (the) Heaven(s) is set up. The saints shall rule the world with the Messiah.

More of this Little Horn is revealed in Chapter 8, concerning the time of his rise to power, the nature of his rule, and the nature of his end.

The Book of Daniel

Chapter VIII

This great chapter is a fuller prophecy on the history and future of two of the empires described in Chapter 7.

The time of the vision is stated to be in the third year of the reign of Belshazzar; no doubt this was near the close of his reign. The Scriptures state that in this vision Daniel is living in the palace of Shushan (Susa), which was located in the Province of Elam. Shushan later became the capital of the Persian Empire. The Ulai is the river Eulaeus.

Now Daniel's prophecy is written in Hebrew again. The prophecy written in Chapter 8 has nothing to do with the Babylonian Empire, so that language is discarded, of course, by Inspiration.

I. *The Vision* (Read verses 1-14).

Daniel sees a Ram which has two horns (one being higher than the other), pushing westward, and northward, and southward, conquering everything in its path. It did not push eastward, of course, because that was from whence it came.

Then a He Goat comes upon the scene with such speed that his feet seem not to touch the ground. There is only One Notable Horn between his eyes. He at once engages the Ram in conflict, breaking its two horns. No one is able to deliver the Ram out of the way of the He Goat. The He Goat continues his exploits until the Notable Horn is broken, and Four Notable Ones come up in its place.

Then out of one of these Four Notable Ones comes a Little Horn, which waxes great toward the south, and toward the east, and toward the pleasant land (Israel). In which direction did he not wax great? — the north. This is the location from whence the Little Horn arises.

This Little Horn bears watching, for it cast down some of the stars from heaven. Truly, it's a supernatural person doing a supernatural act. It is he who magnifies himself to be as God, causing the daily sacrifice to cease for a period of two thousand and three hundred days (this being better translated. "two thousand and three hundred mornings and evenings").

II. *The Interpretation* (Read verses 15-27).

There are three things to remember when interpreting prophecy:
1. The writer many times gives his own interpretation.
2. Facts of history sometimes give the interpretation.
3. Later revelation may give the interpretation.

In Chapter 8 the writer and history both give us the interpretation.

Beginning with verse 15 the writer, Daniel, by inspiration of the Holy Spirit, leaves no doubt as to who these two creatures are. The Ram with Two Horns is stated to be the Media-Persia Empire. The Two Horns correspond with the Two Arms of Silver in Chapter 2 and the Bear who has Two Sides in Chapter 7. The defeat of Media-Persia is predicted, and history bears out this accomplishment through the next creature.

The He Goat is said to be Greece, and the Notable Horn is the first king of Greece — who, of course, turned out to be Alexander the Great. It is told that when Alexander the Great was on his campaign of world conquest, that a Jewish scribe met him and showed him where he was mentioned in the Book of Daniel; thus, he spared the Land of Israel. Alexander the Great is predicted to be cut off, and in his place Four Notable Horns are to arise. History again comes in to relate that Alexander the Great was cut off at a very young age; he died in a drunken debauch in Nebuchadnezzar's former palace. He left an infant son, but the army and people of Greece were reluctant to reserve the throne for this son; therefore, his kingdom was divided between his four generals.

The He Goat with the One Notable Horn corresponds with the Belly of Brass of Chapter 2, and the Four Horns which take the place of the One Notable Horn correspond to the Leopard with Four Heads of Chapter 7.

The names of Alexander the Great's four generals and the territory which was divided unto them are the following:
1. Ptolemy—and to him was given Egypt, Cyrene, Goele-Syria, and the southern parts of Asia Minor.

2. Lysimachus—and to him was given Thrace, parts of Bithynia and Phrygia, Lydia and Mysia.
3. Cassander—and to him was given Macedon and Greece.
4. Seleucus—and to him was given the remainder of Alexander's kingdom, from the river Euphrates to the river Indus; at one time it included the whole of Asia Minor.

Everything which was predicted concerning the Four Notable Horns taking the place of the One Notable Horn came to pass. Now we come to the Little Horn which arises out of one of these Four Notable Horns.

We believe that the Little Horn of Chapter 8 is the same Little Horn of Chapter 7. There are many who will point out, and perhaps rightly so, that the Little Horn of Chapter 7 arises out of the Fourth Beast (Rome), while the Little Horn of Chapter 8 arises out of the Third Beast (Greece). By carefully reading the following verses in Chapter 8, we notice that these Four Notable Horns shall also be existing in the last days, and that the Little Horn rises out of one of these in those days — "... **the time of the end** shall be the vision" (verse 17); "... **in the last end** of the indignation: for at the time appointed the **end shall be**" (verse 19); "And in the **latter time** of their kingdom ..." (verse 23).

These Scriptures clearly point to the fact that these same four territories which were divided among the four generals of Alexander the Great shall be existing in the last days, and we want to point out the fact that they **are** existing today!

That portion of Asia Minor which was the kingdom of Lysimachus, known now as Turkey, became a sovereign state in 1299. The dominion of Seleucus, which today is called Iran (Persia), became a sovereign state in 1794. Cassander's old kingdom of Greece regained its sovereignty in 1830, and the last of the four (Egypt, which was given to Ptolemy) became a sovereign state on October 22, 1930.

These four countries are to be existing in the last days, and the Little Horn is to rise out of one of these. Do you not see that the place of the birth of the Little Horn is now being set up? Truly, his rise is soon; he may be living today.

The Little Horn is no one else but the Antichrist! He shall arise out of one of the four kingdoms, the one which is of the north at the time of this prophecy — Syria. Keep your eye

upon this country of Syria, also Iraq. Iraq and Syria used
to be united; out of this territory comes the Little Horn —
the **Antichrist!**

The Little Horn arises in the last days. We can see
where Antiochus Epiphanes was a forerunner of the Little
Horn. This man did profane the Temple before the time of
the Messiah by offering a sow upon the brazen altar; and
he did cause the sacrifices to cease, but he did not exist in
the last days. Those days are yet to come.

The Little Horn shall cause the daily sacrifices to cease.
Israel, remember, is to be back in the land in the end time
(she is located there now) and will receive animal sacrifices
in her rebuilt temple. From other portions of the Word we
learn that he will confirm a covenant with Israel for seven
years, but after three and one-half years he will break
this covenant with them. For the first three and one-half
years of the Tribulation, known as the 70th Week of
Daniel (see Chapter 9), everything shall be glorious for
Israel; but when the Antichrist (the Little Horn) breaks the
covenant, he causes the sacrifice to cease. In Chapter 9 we
develop the meaning of the abomination of desolation. The
Little Horn, who rises in the last days, shall cause the sacrifices to cease for "two thousand and three hundred days"
(verse 14). Again we point out that a better translation is
"two thousand and three hundred **mornings and evenings.**"
Hence, when the translators first came across these words,
they reasoned that a morning and evening make a day, so
they translated it "days." The question in mind is, "How long
shall the sacrifices cease by reason of the Antichrist?" The
answer given is **two thousand and three hundred morning
and evening sacrifices!** Every day two burnt offerings were
made — one in the morning, and one in the evening (known
also as the morning and evening oblations). There were two
thousand and three hundred morning and evening sacrifices;
and there were two each day; therefore, by dividing the
number of mornings and evenings by two, you have the
correct number of days; divide 360 (the number of days in
the Jewish year) into 1,150 days, you will find how long
the sacrifices will cease — 3 years, 2 months, and 10 days,
nearly the three and one-half years of the last half of the
70th Week of Daniel (the Tribulation). These days do not
fully complete the whole 70th Week of Daniel. No, the
Lord Jesus in Matthew 24:22 says that those days shall be

shortened — "And except those days should be shortened, there should no flesh be saved: but for the elect's sake those days shall be shortened."

Yes, the Little Horn (the Antichrist) shall be "mighty," but not by his own power (verse 24). That power shall be given to him by Satan (see Revelation 13), and he shall be indwelt by Satan himself. A number of the stars are his, and by the power of Satan he will cast them upon the earth. The stars, we believe, are the third of the host of heaven who have followed Satan and who shall be at the disposal of the Antichrist.

But his end shall come, and that occurs when he contacts the Messiah, the Prince of princes, in battle at Armageddon. 'Twill be the conflict of the ages — the Seed of the Woman (Christ) versus the seed of the Serpent (Antichrist). The Antichrist's end shall be in the lake of fire, as we learn in the 19th Chapter of Revelation.

Praise the Lord, God is still on His throne!

The Book of Daniel

Chapter IX

While Chapters 2, 7 and 8 have to do with the Gentile nations, Chapter 9 speaks of Israel from the time of Daniel to that of Christ; then it is silent concerning the Church Age; and then it continues with the rise of the Antichrist.

I. *Reading Israel's Judgment* (Read verses 1-2).

Not only was Daniel, a prophet of God, used as an instrument to reveal the things of the future, but he was a firm believer in the prophecy of the past prophets of God.

Israel was warned of God through Moses (Deuteronomy 28) that judgment would be poured out upon the nation if it should forget God or God's Law. Blessings would be theirs if they obeyed Him, but cursings would be theirs if they disobeyed Him. Here they were in the land of their enemies —proof that they had broken His covenant—as a judgment.

At this time Daniel was reading the prophet Jeremiah who prophesied the Babylonian exile, and not only the exile, but the duration thereof — 70 years (Jeremiah 25:11, 12). They had been in Babylon nearly 70 years now, and Daniel **knew** that it was about time for Israel to go home. In like manner, when we read of the time which characterizes the end of this age, we cannot help but know that it is about time to go **Home!**

II. *Confessing Israel's Sins* (Read verses 3-19).

Daniel takes God's side against Israel, and consequently against himself, as he acknowledges God's justice in meting out His punishment.

He readily admits that the Laws of God were broken by the people of God, and with sorrow of heart he acknowledges how shamefully the prophets were treated. Summing it up, he appeals to the mercy of God for forgiveness. He does not appeal to God on the grounds of Israel's righteousness, because she had none. The mercy of God is the only appeal that a sinner can make to God,

Three times a day this prophet had prayed with his face toward Jerusalem, the City of God, the place of the sanctuary of God. True, the city and the temple were nothing but piles of rubble; they were burned and destroyed. And in this prayer to his God he begs the Lord to visit Israel again and to let His glorious face shine upon His city and its sanctuary.

III. *Unveiling Israel's Future* (Read verses 20-27).

While he was cleansing himself by confession, God sent unto him the angel, Gabriel, to reveal the days of Israel ahead, to give them hope and to assure them of security again. The Lord used this same angel about 500 years later to announce to Zachariah that he was to be the father of John the Baptist, the forerunner of the Messiah. Following this, Gabriel appeared unto the Virgin Mary (Isaiah 7:14) to reveal that she was God's choice to conceive and bear the Messiah!

For 70 years Israel was punished in exile; now God reveals that for 70 weeks Israel would continue, until the golden age of Messianic rule.

The literal Hebrew states that the 70 weeks are "70 sevens." Consequently, the translators assumed that "seven" meant a week (7 days) and translated it as such. But this word "seven" is the same term as used in Genesis, which states that Jacob worked a "seven" for Leah, and then labored another "seven" for Rachel. These "sevens," we know, were **YEARS**. True, we know that the meaning of the "70 sevens" — 70 x seven years — equals 490 years; therefore, 490 years were determined upon Daniel and his people. Israel, for at the end of the 490 years the Messiah would set up the Kingdom.

For 490 years from the time of Solomon Israel did not keep the Sabbatical Year (every seventh year was to be kept holy, as well as the seventh day — no planting, nor gathering of grain or fruit); consequently, there were 70 years during which the land had no rest; God then sent Israel into the Babylonian exile for 70 years to let the land rest. Now, after 490 years from the time of Daniel to the Messiah's enthronement, God will give Israel a thousand (1,000) years of Sabbaths.

Let us try to make these "sevens" as clear as we can.

1. Seventy Weeks (70 sevens; 70 x 7 equals **490** Years) are determined **upon Israel** to finish the transgression, to make an end of sins, and to anoint the most Holy — the Messiah. Four hundred ninety years and the Messiah would start to reign.

2. Seven Weeks (7 x 7), three score weeks (60 x 7), and two weeks (2 x 7) — (49 plus 420 plus 14 equals 483 years) is the time which elapses between the command to build back Jerusalem (Nehemiah 2) unto the Messiah. Then Messiah (the Lord Jesus Christ) was to be cut off. True to this prediction, the Lord Jesus was slain on the cross exactly 483 years after the command was given to restore the city.

3. Three score (60 x 7) and two weeks (2 x 7) (420 plus 14 equals 434 years) elapse from the time Jerusalem is built to the execution of the Messiah.

4. Seven (7 x 7 equals 49 years) weeks lay between the time of the command to build Jerusalem and the time it was finished.

5. Adding them, it took 49 years (7 weeks) to build the city, plus 434 years (60 weeks plus 2 weeks) from the completion of the city to the "cutting off of the Messiah" (483 years).

6. One week (seven years) now remains! After Messiah was cut off (the Lord Jesus crucified), did that 70th Week (seven years) continue? If it did, then we are in the Kingdom now; the Lord Jesus is sitting upon King David's throne in Jerusalem, and sin is at an end.

We can safely say that the Kingdom has not been set up as yet. The Lord Jesus is now sitting upon His HEAVENLY FATHER'S throne but will soon sit upon His own Messianic throne (Revelation 3:21).

What happened between the 69th Week (483rd year) and the 70th Week (the last remaining seven years)? The Church Age is that gap, the valley in between the first coming of Messiah and the second coming of Messiah. As we know, the Church Age was never revealed in the Old Testament but it was known in the mind of God before the foundation of the world (Ephesians 1:4). It was a mystery hid in God and now revealed unto His apostles and prophets (Ephesians 3:1-10). As far as Israel was concerned, it was as though God had punched the stop watch for her after the 483rd year; it was time out then for Israel, and it has lasted for nearly 2,000 years; but as soon as this Church Age is over (the fulness of the Gentiles) the stop watch is punched for Israel again, and Israel is to have the remaining 70th Week (last seven years, known as the Tribulation).

With this in mind let us consider Daniel 9 as he tells us what shall happen during the 70th Week (the last seven years of the Tribulation). Daniel 9:26 states, "Messiah shall be cut off, but not for himself" — right then, the stop watch is punched and the Church Age is ushered in. After the Church Age is over and the gap is closed, the 70th Week of Daniel commences and God turns His attention to Israel — "the people of the prince that shall come shall destroy the city and the sanctuary . . ." Some have applied these words to the destruction of the city and temple in 70 A.D., by Titus. We certainly can apply them to Titus, but the meaning is that the armies of the Antichrist shall destroy the rebuilt temple during these last three and one-half years.

The prince, the Antichrist, shall confirm a seven-year covenant (recognized as the Mosaic Covenant) with Israel. In the midst of that seven-year agreement he breaks his covenant, places his throne in the temple and causes the world to worship him as God (2 Thessalonians 2:1-12); then he shall immediately destroy it.

The elevation to deity and the recognition of worship (in the temple) is the "abomination of desolation" which is referred to by the Lord Jesus in Matthew 24:15.

After the Tribulation (70th Week) is over, Messiah shall return and set up His Kingdom and He shall reign over the whole world.

The Book of Daniel

Chapter X

In this portion of the Book of Daniel we see that the prophet is concerned mostly with himself. Nothing is given us concerning future events except that the "prince of Grecia" is mentioned, which points to the next government which shall arise after the kingdom of Media-Persia has fallen.

However, we do learn something enlightening in this chapter concerning the doctrine of prayer and the doctrine of angels.

I. *Fasting and Prayer* (Read verses 1-12).

Throughout the Old Testament Scriptures we see the development of prayer. Men prayed at the beginning when God manifested Himself in His theophanies; Daniel made a practice of praying three times daily with his face toward the holy city of Jerusalem. Today we are not to pray any less; we are told to pray without ceasing.

Some men fast because they are ill; food cannot be forced into their mouths. Others fast because of poverty; they cannot afford the simplest of foods; yes, there are people living in America today who have never known the satisfaction of having a full stomach. Then there are those who fast, who do without food in order to put first things first — to pray, and pray, and pray! Their hearts are very heavy; food must be forgotten in the face of extremity.

Fasting and prayer is encouraged when one finds himself **alone,** when there is no one to turn to but God!

II. *Hindrances and Deliverances* (Read verses 13-21).

These verses enlighten the believer as to why his prayers are not always answered immediately. God does hear and answer prayer, but sometimes our prayers are not answered as quickly as we think they should be. If God is delaying in answering your prayers, remember this — He may delay, but He is never late.

Many times our sins keep God from answering our prayers; we know when we sin. In I Peter 3:7 we learn that a family's prayers may not be answered because husband and wife are not considering each other. Not praying according to the will of God keeps our prayers from being answered (I John 5:14, 15).

In the life of Daniel we find no mention of sin; yet, he had prayed for twenty-one days and his prayers had not been answered. However, an angel appears unto him and declares that the very first day he prayed his prayers had been heard, and that this angel had been sent to answer them. What caused the delay? The prince of the kingdom of Persia withstood this angel for the twenty-one days and he couldn't get through to Daniel. A call for heaven's help was made and Michael, the archangel, was sent to his rescue and subdued the prince.

What is this all about? Who is the prince of Persia? We believe him to be an angel of great power who has followed Satan, whom Satan has placed as the demoniacal head of this government. From other portions of the Scriptures we learn that Satan is well organized and that he has many of the former angels of God following him, willing to exalt him to a place over God (Ephesians 6:12). This world lies in the hands of the wicked one (I John 5:19), Satan, and he sees to it that his angels are connected with all governments. In verse 20 God shows that when Greece shall come upon the scene, it too shall have an angel appointed over it by Satan.

Michael, the archangel, defeats the prince of Persia, allowing this other angel to come to answer Daniel's prayers. As Satan has his angels set up to defeat the child of God, so the Lord has His guardian angels over His children. The lesson we derive from this encounter of the good and the bad angels is that because of this Satanic conflict our prayers may be delayed in being answered as quickly as they should. But child of God, keep on praying; God may delay, but He is never late. Should there be Satanic forces delaying the answer to your prayers, Michael, or another angel, will come to the rescue.

While angels are sent forth to minister to those who are the heirs of salvation, we are never commanded to pray to **them!**

Michael is the deliverer of God's people; he contended

with Satan over the body of Moses; he shall fight with Satan and his angels, casting them out of heaven in the middle of the Tribulation (Revelation 12:7-10); and he shall deliver God's people out of his hands during the Great Tribulation (Daniel 12:1).

Enoch walked with God; Abraham was called the Friend of God; David was called a Man after God's Own Heart. Here in verse 19 Daniel is called the one Greatly Beloved. What a title! — to be one pointed out by God as one whom He loves.

Looking at verse 21 we are told that Daniel would be given portions of the Word of God that were already written. When were the Scriptures written, and where? "For ever, O LORD, thy word is settled in heaven" (Psalm 119:89). The Scriptures have been written from all time and eternity in heaven. God has allowed His prophets to give us that which has already been recorded in heaven.

The Book of Daniel

Chapter XI

We believe that Chapter 11 belongs to Chapter 10, for verse 14 of Chapter 10 states, "Now I am come to make thee understand what shall befall thy people in the latter days: for yet the vision is for many days." The rest of Chapter 10 tells nothing concerning Israel during the latter days, but Chapter 11 does.

Now as we begin to study this great Chapter 11 we notice that as far as the nations go it is very much like Chapter 8, giving to us the nations of Media-Persia and Greece; then comes the silence of the Church Age, which is skipped over without a hint; the reign of the Anti-Messiah, or Antichrist follows. As far as the Anti-Messiah, or Antichrist, is concerned, it is much like Chapter 9, except that it goes into more detail concerning this vile person who rules this world for three and one-half years during the Great Tribulation.

I. *The Media-Persia Empire* (Read verses 1, 2).

Daniel addresses this great chapter to Darius, the king of Media. It does not only concern this king and his kingdom, the Gentile rulers and rule as well, but it also concerns the life of Israel in the end time. Daniel revealed to Darius that there shall be three kings over Persia following Darius; after their reign the kingdom of Greece arises.

II. *The Grecian Empire* (Read verses 3-20).

The "mighty king," we believe, is no other than Alexander the Great. When he is cut off his kingdom is divided among his four generals (see Chapter 8); it is not left for his small infant son — "and not to his posterity."

After the division of the Grecian Empire among Alexander's four generals, things arise, such as a revolution in one place and a rebellion in another. From verse 5 to verse 20 we have history revealed before it occurs; it is from the time of the Grecian Empire until the time of the Roman Empire. Then there is silence.

We cannot ignore verse 14, and we emphasize again that God wants to tell us more of the things which are going to happen to Israel; we are led to believe they will occur during the Great Tribulation. When the rapture of the Church takes place God's attention is again directed to His ancient people, Israel. Daniel, himself, admits that as he hears and writes this prophecy he does not know what God means by it all; this shows true inspiration. He is told in Chapter 12, verse 9, "Go thy way, Daniel: for the words are closed up and sealed till the time of the end." God clearly tells Israel, and us, that these truths are sealed until the end time. It is true that this great Book of Daniel has become increasingly clear as the years have rolled by. Have you ever read what other commentaries of a hundred years ago, or even two hundred years ago, have had to say about the prophecies of Daniel? They all believed that these Scriptures referred to the Church only, that Israel had been forever forsaken, and that Israel would never be called back to the land of Palestine. But look at the Book of Daniel now! As each year passes another hidden truth comes to light, and we wonder why we haven't seen it before. This great Book shall become more clearly understood as we approach the last days. But greater truths shall be revealed when the last days — the Tribulation — the 70th Week of Daniel — is ushered in. Those Israelites who remain upon the earth to go through the Tribulation will find solace and strength in this Book. We believe that the Book of Daniel, the Book of Revelation, the Old Testament Prophecies, and especially the Gospel of Matthew will serve as **"blue prints"** for Israel during the 70th Week of Daniel. What glorious truths shall be revealed through these Scriptures, especially through the Book of Daniel; by reading them, therefore, they will be able to escape the persecutions of the Anti-Messiah (Antichrist).

III. *The Gap Recognized.*

The Gap (the Church Age) cannot be found in the Old Testament Scriptures (Ephesians 3:1-10). As one reads the Old Testament, he can see the first coming of the Messiah and the second coming of the Messiah, as though it were continuous. But we know that after Messiah was cut off (cruci-

fied), time in the Old Testament ceased. It has ceased until
the Church Age is consummated (Romans 11:25). When this
is accomplished, then time in the Old Testament commences
again. Verse 21 of this 11th Chapter is the point where time
in the Old Testament for Israel begins again.

IV.   *The Little Horn Empire* (Read verses 21-45).

Here is this Anti-Messiah (Antichrist) again! He is the
Little Horn of Chapters 7 and 8 who shall come into power
peaceably (unexpectedly) — and by flatteries (intrigues and
cunningly hypocritical conduct). With an army likened unto
a flood he sweeps everything away in his path. The masses of
the people are swayed by a very few number who rally to
him. How true this has been in our lifetime; dictators rose
to power through the efforts of only a very few.

As we studied Chapter 2 we noticed that the Ten Toes
of Iron and Clay clearly portrayed the Anti-Messiah's rule
through his Ten chosen Kings (see Revelation, Chapter 17).
The kingdom shall possess the strength of Iron of the Old
Roman Empire; yet, it shall be mixed with Clay, the rule
of the people. Clay and Iron cannot mix; therefore, the
Empire shall be partly strong and partly broken. The King
of the South during this time, we believe, is the King of
Egypt. Egypt is now revived (see Chapter 8) after lying
dormant for hundreds of years. Both the King of Egypt and
the Anti-Messiah shall line up for battle and then form a
truce table; but one tries to promise greater things than the
other in order to cover up the deceit of his lies.

The end of these two kings is determined, for God has
decreed it. A short time elapses and they face each other
again, but the ships of Chittim shall cause either a naval
defeat for the Anti-Messiah, or they will discourage him from
going on in this direction. Who is Chittim? From history and
from the Scriptures we are led to believe that Chittim is the
country furthest from Palestine. Wouldn't it be wonderful
if America should be Chittim, the one who stops the progress
of the Anti-Messiah?

Anti-Messiah returns to his own land (Israel) to deceive
the Jewish people all the more. He has made a covenànt
with them (see Chapter 9) for seven years, but now he is
about to break that covenant after only three and one-half

years have elapsed He takes in the leaders of Israel, both religious and political, who in turn deceive the people in acclaiming him to be the Messiah — yea, God Himself! Daily sacrifices are dispensed with, he is enthroned in the Temple and demands to be worshipped. Great masses of the Jewish people follow their leaders and bow to this imposter, the Anti-Messiah. But, praise the Lord, there shall be those who will refuse to bow to this false Messiah. Many of these shall be killed, paying with their lives for refusing to worship him.

The Anti-Messiah shall exalt himself above God, saying that he is God (2 Thessalonians 2). To those who worship him he shall appear as the Lamb, but God calls him the Beast. He shall declare himself to be the Truth, but God calls him the Lie. He shall claim to be the Life, but God declares him to be Death.

We believe that he shall be a Jew, for the Scriptures state that he shall not regard the God of his fathers; this can only be spoken of a Jew. The Gentiles do not know who the God of their fathers was; the Jew knows — He is Jehovah! Knowing and loving the Jewish people as we do, we know they would not accept a Goy (Gentile) as their Jewish Messiah.

He separates himself from women and regards the gods of force. He places his faith in his weapons and relies on the strength of Satan for his power (see Revelation 13).

While the world kingdom of the Anti-Messiah remains partly strong and partly broken, yet we know that the world has been conquered by him, except for the King of the North, which we believe to be Russia and her satellites. In this chapter we learn that he goes to battle against the King of the North. According to Ezekiel 38 and 39, the King of the North and his armies cover Israel as a great cloud. The King of the North is defeated (in Ezekiel 38 and 39 — God is stated to do most of it) and the Antichrist builds his palace between the Mediterranean and the Dead Sea, demanding homage and tribute. His end shall come when, with the Kings of the East (Revelation 9:16; 16:12), he battles the True Messiah, **the Lord Jesus,** at Armageddon.

The Book of Daniel

Chapter XII

This final chapter concludes God's revelation to this greatly beloved prophet concerning His people, Israel.

"At that time" marks the time of the rule of the Anti-Messiah during the last half of the 70th Week of Daniel (see Chapter 9), known as the Great Tribulation. This 12th Chapter speaks of the Tribulation and the Resurrection

I. *The Great Tribulation* (Read verse 1).

We know that this shall be the fiercest of all of the persecution Israel has ever endured. Oh, praise the Lord for those Jewish people who have believed and for those who shall believe and accept the Lord Jesus as their Messiah and Saviour **NOW,** for those who do believe in Him shall escape the coming Tribulation (I Thessalonians 5:9; Revelation 3:10).

We have already seen that a great leader of men shall arise and confirm a covenant with Israel for seven years. During those first three and one-half years Israel shall indeed prosper, even to the erecting of her Temple; she will enjoy perfect harmony and tranquility. But alas, this man breaks the covenant (see Chapter 9), claims to be God, and then destroys the Temple. Israel shall be the object of his persecution, although he, himself, shall be a Jew (see Chapter 11).

The angel, Michael, again shall be called upon to deliver the people of God. And as the Lord Jesus has said, those days shall be shortened for the elect's sake. If they weren't all flesh would die (Matthew 24:21, 22).

II. *The Resurrection* (Read verses 2, 3).

Here the resurrection is stated to occur **AFTER** the Tribulation, while the Church (the Body of the Messiah) shall have its resurrection **BEFORE** the Tribulation begins (I Thessalonians 1:10; 5:9; Revelation 3:10).

Is this a contradiction? — No. Remember, the Old Testament prophets knew nothing of the Church, nor of its Age (which has lasted nearly 2,000 years). When the resurrection is mentioned in the Old Testament, as it is here in the 2nd and 3rd verses, the resurrection of the church is omitted. The resurrection of the **SAINTS,** as recorded in the Old Testament, includes those who have been saved from Adam to the ascension of Christ and those who are saved and die during the Tribulation; it occurs AFTER the Tribulation, while the Resurrection of the Church (as stated before) occurs BEFORE the Tribulation.

There are two resurrections plainly stated in the Scriptures:

1. The resurrection of the saved.
2. The resurrection of the lost (John 5:28, 29).

The resurrection of the saved is called the **first** resurrection (Revelation 20:5); the resurrection of the lost is accepted as the **last** resurrection.

The **first** resurrection is divided into four parts, which are easily recognized:

   a. The Resurrection of Jesus, the Messiah — called the First Fruits.
   b. The Resurrection of the Church — accepted as the Harvest (before the Tribulation).
   c. The Resurrection of the two Witnesses (Revelation 11:11, in the middle of the Tribulation).
   d. The Resurrection of the Old Testament and Tribulation saints — both (c) and (d) recognized as the Gleanings (after the Tribulation).

There is the promise for those who love and win souls to the Messiah; they shall shine as the stars for ever and ever!

III. *The Great Tribulation* (Read verses 4-12).

The Book (or Scroll) is to be sealed until the time of the end — to the time of the Great Tribulation. Yes, man shall increase in his wisdom, but his knowledge of God shall be lacking. This great Book of Daniel shall be the last warning, especially to Israel, during the coming Tribulation, before Messiah returns.

The question is asked, "How long shall it be from the time of the intense persecution of Israel unto the end?" The answer is, "**A time** (one year), **times** (two years), and **one-half time** — three and one-half years altogether." During this terrible time there shall be those who will not bow to the Anti-Messiah, but through these testings they shall come out pure and clean and without a fault. However, the wicked shall increase their wickedness, consenting unto Anti-Messiah and his wishes.

Truly, the last portions of this section shall be clearly seen as the Time of End occurs. Here are two numberings of days:

1. 1,290   2.   1,335; there is a difference of 45 days. From the time the daily sacrifice is taken away to the end of the Anti-Messiah's reign is 1,290 days. There is a blessing offered for those who are able to be present at the end of the 1,335 days. Hence, as we read the 24th Chapter of Matthew, we learn of the purging and judging of Israel — of those Jewish people who come out of the Great Tribulation alive. Matthew 24:37-42 clearly states that when Messiah (the Lord Jesus) appears after the Great Tribulation, He shall judge His people; those who believe not shall be taken to judgment and death (just as when the flood came and took unbelievers away to death at the time of Noah), while those who are believers in the Messiah shall be allowed to remain and go into the golden age of Messiah's millennium. We are thus led to believe that the purging and judging of Israel will take these 45 days. And he who shall endure unto the end (these 45 days) shall be saved (Matthew 24:13).

IV. *The Resurrection* (Read verse 13).

The last verse of Daniel assures the prophet of his own resurrection. He, like all Old Testament saints and dead Tribulation saints, shall have his resurrection at the end of the days — end of the Tribulation. He shall stand in his lot —that portion of land apportioned to his tribe (his family) after he is raised from the dead. Here he was in Babylon, a captive, never again to see his beloved land in this life, but fully guaranteed that he would not only see his native Israel, but would live there under his own vine and fig tree after the resurrection.

Truly, this is a blessed promise to the prophet, yet it is an earthly one. What a contrast there is for the one (Jew or

Gentile) who accepts the Lord Jesus today as Messiah and Saviour! Our blessings are heavenly and spiritual: "Blessed be the God and Father of our Lord Jesus Christ, who hath blessed us with all spiritual blessings in heavenly places in Christ" (Ephesians 1:3). Added to this blessing is the promise that we shall be with the Lord Jesus forever!

The Book of Revelation
Introduction

The word "revelation" means unveiling; thus, this Book is the Unveiling of the Lord Jesus Christ.

The time of the unveiling can be set by verse 7 of Chapter 1 — "He cometh with clouds," which is the Second Coming of Christ (after the Tribulation) to the earth. The Book of Revelation describes the coming of Christ in its two phases:

1. When Christ comes for His saints (Chapters 4 and 5).

2. When Christ comes with His saints (Chapter 19).

Between the two phases is the Tribulation. The first half of the Tribulation (first 3½ years) is portrayed in Chapters 6-11, while the second half of the Tribulation (last 3½ years) is noted in Chapters 12-19.

Chapter 1, verse 19, is the KEY to the Book, "Things which thou has seen" (Past); "Things which are" (Present); and "Things which are to come" (Future).

Past: Chapter 1; Present: Chapters 2, 3; Future: Chapters 4-22.

The Book of Revelation
Chapter I

Many have thought that this great Book is the revelation of John, but verse 1 clearly tells us that it is the revelation (unveiling) of the Lord Jesus Christ.

I. *The Revelation of Christ to His Servants* (Read verses 1-3).

How perfect in detail the Holy Spirit composes the Scriptures. The very word "servants" is an inclusive word. We know that this great Book is to and for the Church, but believing that the Church is raptured in Chapters 4 and 5, how could it be to the Church when the Church will not be here? This proves that this Book is not just for the Church, but it is also for the servants," those believers who shall live in the Tribulation, who were not believers when the rapture of the Church occurred. This is one portion of Scripture which promises blessings to those who read it and to those who hear and obey it.

II. *The Revelation of Christ for His Servants* (Read verses 4-8).

He called the Witness, yea, the true One, the First begotten from the dead; He was the first to be raised from the dead never to die again. He is the coming Prince, or Ruler. the Saviour who washed us from our sins by His matchless blood. He is stated to be the Coming One; He is the Alpha and the Omega — the A through Z — the Beginning and the Ending — He is All! Amen.

Those who say He never claimed to be divine and that He never claimed to be God should read what He calls Himself here — the ALMIGHTY — El Shaddai the Almighty God — the God who is sufficient — the God who is enough! Amen.

He is associated with the seven Spirits, whom many think to be a term given to the third person of the Trinity, the

Holy Spirit (Isaiah 11:2). Yet, in later chapters we find seven spirits attending him as he sits upon the throne.

III. *The Revelation of Christ by His Servant* (Read verses 9-20).

This servant is John, who 66 years before had leaned upon the breast of Christ at the Passover. He was a young man then, but is now the aged one, whose heart still overflows with love for his Lord.

Verse 9 states that he is the companion of those who were suffering for Christ during the time of the writing, which he calls **the Tribulation.** We know this is not speaking of the 70th Week of Daniel — the Tribulation which is termed Jacob's Trouble in Jeremiah 30:6, 7, but rather of the Church Age, which is called by Paul in Colossians 1:24 "the afflictions of Christ"; it is better translated as the "tribulations of **the** Christ," the Church.

John was upon the isle of Patmos, either to get this great Book, or because he was banished as a national prisoner for preaching the Word (Jesus); and being in this place, he was given the Revelation.

We believe that when he speaks of the Lord's Day he is speaking of the coming Day of the Lord (the day of judgment so often spoken of in the Old Testament) and that he was given an insight of it by the Spirit. Applying the meaning of the term Lord's Day that we use today, it could mean the 1st day of the week — the day which we commemorate as the day on which Christ arose from the dead.

The Lord Jesus appears unto him as John is in the Spirit and he sees the Lord, no doubt, as He appeared upon the Mount of Transfiguration 66 years before. He is standing in the midst of seven candlesticks; rather, seven individual lampstands, with seven stars in His hand. Verse 20 tells us that the seven lampstands are the seven churches of Asia, and the stars are the angels of these seven churches. Angel in the original means deputy, minister, etc.; therefore, we are led to believe that the seven stars are the seven pastors of these seven churches.

Christ appears with white hair, denoting that He is coming as a Judge to judge the world. His eyes are as flames of fire; He is omniscient; He knows and sees all things. A

Sword goeth forth out of His mouth—truly, the Word of God, which can break in pieces as a hammer, cut as a sharp two-edged sword, and burn as a fire. His feet are said to be as burning brass; brass denotes judgment. Thank God, when Christ comes for us at the rapture, He comes as the Bride-groom and not as the Judge. His relation to us in this present age is the Head of His Body; He stands in the **middle** of His Churches — certainly He must be the Hub with all things revolving around Him. He has His ministers, or pastors, in His hands to place and to guard them.

The Book of Revelation
Chapter II

Chapters 2 and 3 are the portions of this Book which deal with the Present — "things which are."

There are five interpretations of these seven churches; four of them have proved correct, and the other can be fulfilled. They are:

1. Seven churches which existed at the time of John.
2. Seven types of local churches.
3. Seven types of Christians.
4. Seven periods of Church History.
5. Seven churches in these cities of Asia which might be existing just before the rapture.

Whatever your interpretation, whether to a local church or to an individual, the truths apply to all.

I. *The Church in Ephesus* (Read verses 1-7).

This is the First Church Age (30-110 A.D.).

The name Ephesus means "desirable" and "let go"; this church and Church Age had a wonderful start in the Lord. They were so sound in their teaching that they drifted into legalism, and before long it was found that the "letter which killeth" was thwarting the Spirit which maketh alive.

The Lord Jesus is Omniscient — He knows all — and He says ,"I know thy works." And He does know our works; He also knows whether they be of the Spirit or of the Law. They had left their first love; they had not lost it; the spirit of their new life was gone; their love for Christ had grown cool in their cold orthodoxy. Lost souls and the winning of them was a lost passion.

Christians (born-again believers) were commanded to repent, to change their minds, which in turn would change their living. Abundant blessings are offered to this Church and to all of the Churches. I John 5:4,5 tell who the OVER-COMERS are — those who have believed completely in the finished work of Christ — His death, burial, and bodily resurrection.

II. *The Church in Smyrna* (Read verses 8-11).

This Church describes the Second Church Age (110 — 315 A.D.)

There is no criticism of this Church. The Omniscient Christ knows their plight and their suffering, for He has experienced it; He Who was **dead** is now **alive!**

The name Smyrna comes from the word Myrrh, the perfumed liquid used in anointing the dead. Consequently, the saints here lived up to the reputation of their city's name; they suffered and died for the cause of the Lord Jesus. Those who died with their faith in Jesus Christ are overcomers, and the overcomers are promised a life which shall never die.

III. *The Church in Pergamos* (Read verses 12-17).

This characterized the Third Church Age (315 - 500 A.D.).

The meaning of Pergamos is "tower" and "marriage." The entire text portrays the marriage of those who called themselves Christians to legal formalism, which truly has developed during the Church Age.

It is the Omniscient Christ who knows all about these people; He compliments them for their faith in not denying His name, while he reprimands those within their ranks who, like those of old, hold to the doctrine of Balaam — tempting the men of God to marry the women of Moab; here it is applied to the union, or marriage, of professing believers to the world; by so doing they lose their separation, etc.

Repent is the watchword — change your minds; stop this sinning and examine yourselves and see whether you be in the faith or not. He who is in the faith and is an overcomer (I John 5:4,5) will be given to eat of hidden manna and will be given a new name written in a white stone. This is also the promise to all believers in Christ.

IV. *The Church in Thyatira* (Read verses 18-29).

This covers the Fourth Church Age (about 500-1500 A.D.).

The meaning of Thyatira is "never tiring of sacrifice." Truly, during this Church Age the continued sacrifice of

Christ upon Church altars, through the Mass, was introduced to the Church. The Scriptures plainly state that Christ Jesus put away sin once and for all by His One offering for sin; yet, since that time we hear that this completed sacrifice is perpetuated upon their altars. What hypocrisy! What blasphemy!

It was Jezebel who introduced Baal worship to the ten tribes of Israel, and it was the organized Church which introduced this form of pagan idolatry into the true Church of Jesus Christ.

The Omniscient Christ points to this sin and demands repentance on the part of those who are believers, but who are being misled into a ritualistic form of worship.

To the overcomer (I John 5:4,5 — the true believer), whether in that Church or in another, is promised the Morning Star (Jesus Christ) and the right to reign with Him.

The messages of Christ to His seven Churches are concluded in Chapter 3.

The Book of Revelation
Chapter III

We continue toward the conclusion of the Lord Jesus' messages to the seven Churches, which covers the second division of the Book of Revelation — "the things that are."

I. *The Church in Sardis* (Read verse 6).

The injunction to this Church fully reveals the Church Age (from 1500 to around 1750 A.D.), commonly known as the Reformation (the Fifth Church Age).

Remember, this is also spoken to a local assembly and is for them individually (as the other six messages) and collectively.

Sardis has several meanings, such as "escaping ones," "who come out," and "remnant." And to those who are very weak, but who come out to believe wholly in the Lord Jesus Christ for their salvation, white garments shall be presented.

The overcomer (I John 5:4,5), of all Church Ages, and in all local Churches, is promised the security that his name shall never be blotted out of the Book of Life. If one is not an overcomer (believer) his name shall be blotted out.

Right here let us state that we believe in the eternal security of the believer, and we believe that the believer's name shall remain forever in the Book of Life. I know more explanation is needed. To begin with we ask, "When were our names recorded in the Book of Life? — at Salvation?" The Scriptures do not state so, but rather that all men's names are recorded there, even before any sinner became a saint (look at Revelation 17:8). All men's names were recorded there from the foundation of the world. David shows us that the names of the wicked are written along with names of the righteous (see Psalm 69:28).

Are names ever blotted out of the Book? Yes, they are; look at Exodus 32:33. Those who had sinned, God said, would be blotted out of His book. **When** were they blotted out? When they died. Now we get the message. All men's names are recorded in the Book of Life, saint and sinner alike. This proves that **no one** is on God's black list. When a man is saved, he becomes an overcomer; his name stays in the Book. If a man dies in unbelief, then his name is blotted out at the time of his death.

II. *The Church in Philadelphia* (Read verses 7-13).

This Church portrays the Sixth Church Age (from 1750-1910 A.D.).

The meaning of Philadelphia is "brotherly love." Search your Church History and the records of your denomination and you will be surprised to learn of the great missionary societies, Bible societies, etc., which were started during these years.

There is no reprimand from Christ, the Omniscient One — He knows all about them. They have a **little** strength in the Lord, and that is all that is required. Before them were set forth doors which no man can shut. What a promise to those of us who have heard the Lord's command to "go." Nothing can stop us; no one can block the way if He has directed.

The Lord Jesus guarantees deliverance to all of His believers from the coming "Hour of Temptation" — the Tribulation. Praise the Lord, the Spiritual blessings include the believers becoming as pillars in His temple, having the names of God and the Temple of God written upon them.

III. *The Church in Laodicea* (Read verses 14-22).

This is the Seventh Church Age.

The meaning of the word Laodicea is "people's rights," and this Church fully tells of the Age we are in now, which began about 1910 and will continue to the Rapture of the Church. The accepted Church is neither cold, nor is it hot. The Lord Jesus says it would be best if we were hot or cold; but, as we are tepid, we make Him sick. He said, "I'll spew thee out of my mouth." There is chastening promised to those who will not come out and live consecrated lives for their Lord.

You will notice that the Lord Jesus stands at the door, about ready to appear to the believer, only, at the close of the

Church (or Church Age). How close He is to us. As we write we cannot help but wonder whether we will be able to finish these messages before He returns.

Spiritually Christ would have us open the doors of our hearts and of our Churches to Him, that we may have sweet communion with Him. To the overcomer (I John 5:4,5) of all ages, the promise to reign with Christ is given. Here the Lord Jesus points out the fact that He is now sitting on His Heavenly Father's throne; and one day will He, with His saints, sit on His own throne.

The Book of Revelation
Chapter IV

Chapter 4 marks the beginning of "things which shall be hereafter" — those things which shall occur after the Church Age.

Chapters 4 and 5 clearly picture to us the Rapture of the Church and the final ceremony of our Redemption.

I. *The Enthroned Lord* (Read verses 1-3).

These verses and verses 9-11 leave no doubt in our minds that the Lord Jesus is the One being spoken of, Who, as the Son of God, is sitting upon the Father's throne. Everything connected with the throne and the Lord Jesus is a spectacle of beauty. The rainbow was a sign given to Noah, promising that God would never destroy the earth again by water. Here in heaven is a beautiful rainbow which is God's promise that He will never destroy those who believe in Him.

II. *The Enthroned Elders* (Read verses 4, 5).

Surrounding the throne of God are twenty-four thrones upon which elders of heaven are sitting. The fact that David had twenty-four elders to help him govern and judge Israel suggests that God uses these elders to govern the affairs of heaven. Remember, when Nebuchadnezzar (see Daniel 4) dreamed of a tree and it was interpreted that he would be cut down and later elevated, it was decreed by the "watchers" in heaven. No doubt, they are these twenty-four elders.

III. *The Exalted Christ* (Read verses 6-11).

Before the throne were four beasts (creatures) and their likenesses were as a lion, an ox, a man, and an eagle. This is similar to the vision that Ezekiel saw of the glory of God (Ezekiel 1). The four Gospels themselves speak of the same. Matthew presents Christ as the Lion — King; Mark describes Him as the Ox — Servant; Luke pictures Him as the perfect man — Man; and John emphasizes Him as the eagle —

God. The Lord Jesus is a composite of all four. While He is King, yet He is Servant; while He is Man, yet He is God.

These creatures glorify the Triune God in worshipping the Lord Jesus, who is the fulness of the Godhead bodily — Father, Son, and Holy Spirit.

Upon worshipping the Lord Jesus the elders at once bow before Him and cast their crowns, which they had won, at the feet of our Adorable Lord. Yes, they had persevered; they had worked for their crowns, but all glory was given to Christ! And may He forever receive the glory for everything!

Verse 11 states plainly that all things were created by and for the pleasure of Him who sitteth upon the throne. Other Scriptures plainly declare that the Lord Jesus is He who created all things, and without Him was not anything made that was made.

Now we go into Chapter 5, which consummates the redemption of mankind.

The Book of Revelation

Chapter V

This wonderful chapter continues where Chapter 4 leaves off. We see Christ sitting upon His Father's throne, sitting there as He is—God! Now we will see His transition from the exalted place of God to that of becoming Man in order to redeem man.

This vision is in heaven, and when we come to Chapter 6 we see that as these things are happening in heaven there are acts of judgment occurring on earth at the same time.

I. *The Enthroned Lord* (Read verses 1-4).

Being God He has the Book (Scroll) of our redemption in His hand. The Scroll is written within and on the backside. By turning to Leviticus 25 we read how a man in olden times could sell himself into slavery, with the provision, however, that he could be bought back and set free. When a man was in need of money, by debt, or otherwise, he could sell himself to a neighbor; when he did the act was recorded within a Scroll. On the backside the provisions were listed as to how he could be redeemed (bought back): (1) the **price,** and (2) by a **near kinsman** (goel). Then the Scroll was sealed with seven seals.

After some time had elapsed and the new slave began to desire his freedom, he would call for a near kinsman—his uncle, brother or nephew. He would ask that one of them buy him back. If the request was honored, the near kinsman would speak to the master. The Scroll would be brought and the near kinsman (goel) would pay the amount that was demanded.

Here in Heaven we find the same situation. The saints are there waiting for the seals of the Scroll of their Redemption to be broken that they might be forever set free. The Scroll, in the hands of the Lord Jesus, is written within and on the backside and sealed with seven seals. Who will be worthy to break them? The Redeemer must be a **NEAR KINSMAN**, and He must have the Redemption Price.

John cries because no man has been found worthy to break the seals.

II. *The Expected Lion* (Read verse 5).

An elder appears to John and assures him they have found ONE Person Who is worthy to break the seals, One Who is a NEAR KINSMAN and Who has the PRICE for the Redemption. He was told that this Person is the Lion of Judah, of the Tribe of Judah — the Root of David. He it is Who hath prevailed. We know Whom this is, don't we? He Who was upon the Throne became the Lion of Judah, the Son of David — the Messiah! Bless His holy name!

III. *The Executed Lamb* (Read verses 6-14).

John turned, expecting to see a Lion, but he saw a Lamb; it was not just a lamb, but a lamb that had been recently slain. It has been nearly 2,000 years since the Lord Jesus, as the Lamb of God, died; and we know that the rapture will take place even after this day; yet, the Lord still bears in His precious body the wounds (not just the scars) from which He died for us.

Here, as in Daniel 7, when the Son of Man comes to the Ancient of Days, the Lamb comes to the throne; it is Jesus, the Son of David, coming to Him Who is Jesus, the Son of God! How could we finite beings see it in any other way than that which is expressed by these words?

It is the Lord Jesus, God manifested in the flesh, Who became the NEAR KINSMAN (the goel)—"he took not on him the nature of angels, but the seed of Abraham" (Hebrews 2:16). Who possessed the Price of sinless blood and a sinless life to lay down as a Substitute for the sins of all mankind? — only God! But God does not have blood and cannot die; therefore, God became flesh so that He could die and so that He could shed sinless blood!

It was upon the Cross that the Lord Jesus paid for our redemption. At the rapture we shall be taken out of the slave market of sin; and at this throne and before this throne, when the Lord Jesus breaks the seals thereof, we shall be set free!

All heaven breaks forth in praise unto the Lord Jesus. Then earth joins in, and even those who are under the earth shall give the Lord Jesus glory! Truly, it is universal acclaim.

As we continue to study this great Book we cannot help but notice that **time** itself flows as do the waves of the sea upon the seashore. Watching as waves come in and cover a stretch of sand, we see one larger wave which overflows the rest and goes farther upon the beach; so it is with this Book of Revelation. In one chapter we cover one age, and in the next chapter we may cover the same time, until one large wave, as it were, carries on past the ages being discussed and reaches way beyond. So it is in this Chapter; universal adoration of Christ will take place after the 1,000 years are over; here it seems that it took place right at the Rapture.

The Book of Revelation
Chapter VI

While heaven is giving attention to the worship of the Lord Jesus and waits for the breaking of the seals, earth is being prepared for the judgments which shall be meted out as each seal is broken. The Vision is one, yet part is in heaven and the other part is on earth. They both happen simultaneously.

I. *Seal One* (Read verses 1, 2).

As the first seal is broken in heaven a judgment is handed to earth. In the original the words "Come, and see" are just "Come." The command is not given to John, but rather to the riders upon these horses. As the first command is given, a man upon a white horse goes out to conquer. We believe him to be the Anti-Messiah (Antichrist). This marks the **beginning** of his rise to power. Remember, Chapters 6-11 have to do with the first three and one-half years of the Tribulation. His complete ascension to the earthly throne is accomplished in the 13th and 17th Chapters.

II. *Seal Two* (Read verses 3, 4).

"Come," or as we would say, "Go," is the command given to the rider on the red horse. This is descriptive of War—peace being taken from the earth. When one goes out to conquer, war is inevitable.

III. *Seal Three* (Read verses 5, 6).

Famine follows closely upon the heels of war, and the command, "Come," is obeyed. Right here we are beginning to see how the earth shall be suffering to produce enough food for all. As it becomes scarce the greater the demand will be for a One-man ruler of the World. Chapters 13 and 17 tell us that this very thing shall happen.

One small wheat pancake for a penny, or three barley pancakes for a penny are the prices asked at this time; this shows how scarce food is going to be. A penny is a **day's wage!** What is your day's wage? In the Tribulation it will buy very little.

In all of the holocaust, the olive trees and vineyards shall be spared, and there shall be an abundance of fruit from both.

IV. *Seal Four* (Read verses 7, 8).

The order, "Come," is obeyed by death and hades (the condition and the place of the dead). By means of war, famine and wild beasts, one-fourth of the earth's population shall be destroyed.

V. *Seal Five* (Read verses 9-11).

There are no more horses or riders, but we are allowed to view the scene of carnage which has been imposed, especially upon the believers.

These verses show clearly those who will be martyred during the first three and one-half years of the Tribulation. They cry for vengeance and are told to rest a little season, for there would be believers, like they, who were to be killed for their faith (See Revelation 20:4).

While they wait under the altar white robes are given them to wear. Describing them as being under the altar is symbolically beautiful. Under the Old Covenant men came to the brazen altar and made their burnt and peace offerings as sweet savour offerings. The blood (life is in the blood) of these animals was caught and poured into a hole prepared at the foot of the altar—the blood thus seeping under the altar. In heaven there is the brazen altar which Moses was commanded to copy after (Hebrews 8:5). Now we see that these people have given their lives as Burnt and Peace offerings to God—yes, sweet savour offerings to the Lord. As the blood of animals was poured at the foot of the altar and their blood was under the altar, so it is that the souls of these martyred saints are placed under God's altar.

VI. *Seal Six* (Read verses 12-17).

In these verses we see, as it were, another wave in the

ocean of time, sweeping from the time the seal is broken on to the end of the Tribulation, when men's hearts shall fail them as they realize that they must face the Lord Jesus Christ. All means are exhausted to hide them from the "wrath of the Lamb." John expected to see a Lion (Chapter 5), but he saw a Lamb; these men shall expect to see a Lamb, but they will see a Lion—the Lamb-Lion—Jesus Christ! The Lord Jesus Christ shall appear after the Tribulation and shall mete out true justice to the ungodly.

The Book of Revelation
Chapter VII

You will notice that Chapter 7 is parenthetical; that is, it has been inserted between the sixth and the seventh seal. How our hearts are made to rejoice over this chapter, for in it we see that much unbelief shall be taken away from Israel and that there shall be a very large number of Gentiles saved, in addition to the Jewish people.

Another thing we learn is that there shall be many believers who shall go through the Tribulation without dying.

I. *The Sealing of Israel* (Read verses 1-8).

More judgment is to be pronounced upon the earth, but before it is to be carried out the servants of God are to be sealed as they go into the Great Tribulation.

Many people have tried to set forth the meaning of the 144,000 who are sealed, but have failed miserably. The Word plainly teaches that they are all **Israelites—Jews!** And 12,000 from each of the 12 Tribes are sealed to be the SERVANTS, which we believe are the preachers during the Great Tribulation.

Whenever the Tribes of Israel are mentioned there are always twelve. We know, however, that Joseph got a double portion in the land through his two sons, Ephraim and Manasses. In these Scriptures Joseph is substituted for Ephraim, but Manasses is called by name. Levi did not get a portion in the Land (for this tribe provided the priests for Israel) as the LORD Himself became Levi's portion. But Levi is mentioned here. There is one tribe omitted, and that is DAN. There are plausible reasons why Dan is omitted: (1) because Dan was the first tribe to go into apostasy in the promised land; (2) the prophecy of Jacob in Genesis 49:17 reveals that, as Dan is the "serpent by the way, an adder in the path," the Anti-Messiah (Antichrist) shall arise from this tribe. Hence, God will not allow any from that tribe to be preachers during the Great Tribulation.

But here is a glorious truth: Dan shall come in for her

portion of the land during the 1,000 year reign of Messiah (Ezekiel 48:1). Praise the Lord! Though the identities of the Tribes of Israel are unknown today (except for the Tribe of Levi), God will identify the tribes from which these precious soul winners will be composed.

II. *The Saving of the Gentiles* (Read verses 9-17).

John is given a vision of a vast multitude that no man could number of all the tribes and nations of the world. He is asked who they may be, but he requests the elder to tell him, for the elder knows. His answer tells us that they are those who go through the Great Tribulation without dying, who have made their robes white by the blood of the Lamb. Here is that precious Lamb again! God would have us never to slight Him nor forget Him.

The Book of Revelation

Chapter VIII

After studying that wonderful Chapter 7, which we found to be parenthetical (sandwiched in between Seal Six and Seal Seven), we commence again with the Seventh Seal.

I. *Seal Seven* (Read verse 1).

One-half hour of silence concludes the ceremony which signifies our completed redemption.

II. *Seven Trumpets* (Read verses 2-13).

We have pointed out before that when Moses was upon Mt. Sinai he was told to copy after the pattern in heaven (Hebrews 8:5); thus, the tabernacle on earth was just a copy of the Tabernacle (Temple) in heaven. Should we pull back the first veil and step inside the Holy Place, we would see on our left the seven-point candlestick; on the right we would see the table of shewbread; in front of us, and stationed right before the Inner Veil, stood the Altar of Incense upon which fresh fire and incense were placed daily. The place of this golden altar was in the Holy of Holies, where the High Priest went in just ONCE a year on the Day of Atonement; but in order to service it daily, it had to be brought out and set in the Holy Place. In heaven, however, the Golden Altar of Incense was placed INSIDE the Holy of Holies right before God.

The burning of incense on earth became a type of the High Priest's prayers of Christ. In heaven the incense is a type of the prayers of the saints — prayers which beseeched the Lord to revenge them of their persecutors. Here in this chapter, with the sounding of the Trumpets, God begins to answer these prayers and it is symbolized with the 8th angel casting fire down upon the earth. Who is this 8th angel? We believe it to be just the 8th angel and not the Lord Jesus, for Jesus is God, sitting down upon the throne in the Holy of Holies.

This is another vision. When the trumpets are being blown in heaven judgment comes to the earth.

As we go into these judgments, take everything as literally as possible, including the rest of the Book of the Revelation. Someone has truthfully said, "When common sense makes good sense, seek no other sense."

A. *Trumpet One* (Read verse 7).

With the sounding of this trumpet in heaven a great judgment of fire is poured upon the earth and one-third of the trees are burned up. This includes the fruit and nut trees. Then all **green grass** (another term for vegetables) is ruined — one year's crop failure. We can begin to see the terrible situation the world is going to be in. Food shall indeed be scarce and the need shall arise for a world food distributor . . . the Anti-Messiah (Antichrist) shall be the one.

B. *Trumpet Two* (Read verses 8, 9).

We have read of happenings in our time as when the top, or even a whole mountain, was destroyed by volcanic eruption. When this does occur the poison derived from it shall kill the third part of the creatures of the sea. What terrible epidemics shall spread over the countries which surround the Mediterranean Sea. We believe this **sea** is the Mediterranean. One-third of the ships shall be destroyed. Look at the Navies of the world and notice where their ships are located. Many are now stationed in this Sea. What a loss it shall be to the Navies of the world and to their war machines.

C. *Trumpet Three* (Read verses 10, 11).

We believe in the literalness of these verses; we believe that such a star shall fall and cause waters to be made bitter. God says that He knoweth the number of stars and calleth them by their names. Here He names **one** (Wormwood) which shall poison the fountain-head of some great sweet water channel.

D. *Trumpet Four* (Read verses 12, 13.)

Take everything as it is and it makes sense. What will happen when the sun and the moon shall fail to shine their full strength? Vegetation shall be smitten all the more. In verse 13 a better translation of the "angel" is **eagle** — a bird;

yes, an eagle shall cry these words. He Who has made other birds speak can certainly cause an eagle to talk. God is using everything possible to get people to believe. We shall continue to study more of the Trumpets in the next chapter.

The Book of Revelation
Chapter IX

Chapter 9 is the continuation of the Trumpets which began in Chapter 8. The sounding of the Fifth and Sixth Trumpets has brought much speculation by teachers of the past, and we shall try to give the sanest interpretation that can be made.

Remember, when we study this great Book of Revelation, the best way to understand it is to take it literally as much as possible.

I. *Trumpet Five* (Read verses 1-12).

When the Trumpet is blown another judgment is poured upon the earth. A "star" falls from heaven. This can be a literal star, for we have already studied about another star which fell, and its name is called "Wormwood" (see Chapter 8). Then, too, we know that letting Scripture interpret Scripture, Satan and his angels are called "stars" (see Daniel 8:10). The following chapters tell us that Satan shall be cast out of heaven (Chapter 12); here in Chapter 9 this star is said to be given the keys to the bottomless pit; rather, a very deep pit. Chapter 11, verse 7, tells of the beast which ascends out of the very deep pit — this person is the Anti-Messiah (Antichrist). Therefore, all things which are cast into the very deep pit (Bottomless), or which come out of it, are Satanic.

Some have interpreted that unto the "star" was given the key to the bottomless pit, while others say that unto the Fifth Angel was given the key. We believe that the key is given to the Fifth Angel, for the plague of locusts which comes out of the pit causes much pain and distress upon the ungodly. Satan certainly would not persecute his own.

The locusts are described as terrible creatures which have the sting of a scorpion; after they sting a man the hurt remains for five months. Men try to take their own lives, but it is of no avail. Death does take a holiday here. Some have believed that they are machines of war, either of the air, or machines of death likened unto present armored tanks.

A missionary from India once told me that in that country they have locusts which are very large and that fulfill the description perfectly, even to long manes and faces that look like men. These could literally be locusts that shall plague the ungodly (the lost) during this time of the Tribulation.

II. *Trumpet Six* (Read verses 13-21).

We believe that this portion of the Scriptures is symbolic, as it describes the creatures of war which shall be employed in the last days.

The River Euphrates is mentioned here, and consequently, keep in mind the city of Babylon, which is brought into focus. We remember from Daniel 5 how this river was used by the Medes and Persians in overthrowing the City of Babylon. Again this well-known river of the East shall be employed in the wars of the last days.

This chapter is the first to mention the 200 million-man Army of the Anti-Messiah (Antichrist). Chapter 16 develops it further by suggesting that they come from the far East. This massive army causes the death of one-third of the world's population at this time. In Chapter 6, verse 8, a fourth of the population has already been destroyed. Then, with this one-third more being killed, there is a total of one-half of the world's population being obliterated. The world leaders today are fearful of the "explosive population" of the world. We see that this "over population" will be well taken care of in the coming Tribulation.

The Book of Revelation
Chapter X

Chapter 10 is another parenthetical chapter of this great Book.

I. *The Angel* (Read verses 1, 2).

This angel is just "another angel." Some have ascribed him to be the Lord Jesus, but we notice in verse 6 that he "sware by him that liveth for ever and ever, who created heaven, and the things that therein are . . ."; this is no one but God, the Son. Hence, this angel is just as these Scriptures describe him to be — "another angel."

II. *The Thunders* (Read verses 3-7).

We have several "sealings" of this great Book: the Book (Scroll) of Chapter 5, with seven seals; the 144,000 Israelites sealed in Chapter 7; those who do not have the seal in Chapter 9; and Satan who is sealed in the very deep pit (Bottomless) in Chapter 20.

Daniel (Daniel 12:4) was told to seal his prophecy until the "time of the end"; however, the Book of Revelation is an **open** Book, but with this exception — the seven thunders. What they said, and the interpretation thereof, is not given. This is the only portion of Revelation that is not revealed. We do not know why.

"That there should be time no longer" (verse 7b) means "there should be no more delay" — so that the Mystery of God should be completed. Paul is one of the New Testament prophets, and it was he who revealed to us the "Mystery of God, even Christ" (Colossians 2:2). The Lord Jesus is that Truth, for He is God manifested in the flesh. Here in Chapter 10, verse 7, we are told that this great truth is about to be completed and that its completion shall begin to take place with the sounding of the Seventh Trumpet (Chapter 11, verse 15), when the Lord Jesus shall return and judge the ungodly (Jude 14; 2 Thessalonians 1:6-11).

III. *The Little Book* (Read verses 8-11).

A better word for "Book," we know, is "scroll." John is commanded to eat the Scroll and he does eat it. He was warned that the taste would be sweet, but that his belly would be made bitter. We have a name for that today — heartburn. We believe the Scroll to be the Word of God. The mouths of those who eat it are indeed made sweet, but the effects are truly bitter. In other words we have to do what we say; we have to practice what we preach. The Words make good preaching, but many times it makes hard living. Israel (Exodus 19:8) proudly declared, "All that the LORD hath spoken we will do." It was easy to **say** that they would obey the LAW, but how hard it was for that nation to actually **obey** the LAW.

John is promised the opportunity to preach to many more governmental officials of his time the contents of this Book.

The Book of Revelation
Chapter XI

In the preceding chapters we have considered the world and its people (with the exception of Chapter 7, the sealing of 144,000 Israelites). Now our attention is focused upon the people of Israel and its capital, Jerusalem.

Verses 1-14 are included in the parenthetical Chapter 10.

I. *The Temple* (Read verses 1, 2).

The Lord Jesus declared that the Temple which was standing at that time would be destroyed, and it came to pass 40 years later; Herod's Temple was destroyed by Titus (70 A.D.).

Other later prophecies, given after our Lord's prediction, declare that the Anti-Messiah (Antichrist) shall place his throne in the Temple and declare himself to be God (2 Thessalonians 2). Consequently, if Herod's Temple is to be destroyed and the Anti-Messiah arises to put his throne in it, a new Temple must be erected. And that is exactly what shall be done. The nation of Israel wants to do that very thing today, but as yet the nation does not own the old site of Jerusalem. Upon the very site of the old Temples (Solomon's, Zerubbabel's, and Herod's) there is today the "Dome of the Rock," a Mohammedan mosque. The Time of the Gentiles is not yet over. However, we believe that the Anti-Messiah (Antichrist), in confirming the covenant with Israel, shall include the provision of the site of the Temples, whereupon Israel shall build this new Temple (many calling it today the Anti-Messiah's (Antichrist) Temple).

This Temple's destruction shall last forty and two months — three and one-half years. This, of course, is the time allotted for the last half of the Tribulation. Hence, we take note that this Temple is destroyed in the middle of the 70th Week of Daniel, the Tribulation.

II. *The Two Witnesses* (Read verses 3-14).

These witnesses have been saved immediately after the

rapture of the Church, for had they been saved before this event, they would have gone up with the Church. They witness to the saving power of the Lord Jesus Christ; thus, they emphasize the New Covenant to the exclusion of the Old Covenant with its animal sacrifices. They preach the Lamb of God as being the sacrifice of the New Covenant. Not only do they witness against the religion of Israel at Jerusalem, but they also testify against the one-world religion of Babylon (see Chapter 17). We know this, for not only does Israel rejoice, but the whole world rejoices to learn of their death.

Who are these witnesses? Some say they are Moses and Elijah, for they are able to do the miracles of Moses and Elijah. Others say they are Enoch and Elijah, for these men never died; thus, God wants every man to die. This does not hold, for in I Corinthians 15:51 we are told that **we** shall not all die. Then, who are they? The best interpretation is that they are just the "Two Witnesses" as prophesied by Zechariah (4:2,3).

"Man is immortal 'til God is through with him" is certainly proven by them. Many schemes are devised to kill them, but they are of no avail until they have "finished their testimony." When this is ended God allows the Anti-Messiah to kill them.

Nineteen hundred years ago, when this prophecy was first read, it caused much distress as to how the **world** could see the dead bodies of these Two Witnesses for three and one-half days. Yea, even during the past two hundred years, ministers of the Gospel have had much difficulty in interpreting these Scriptures. Today, with the sending up of the "Tel-star" (and no doubt many more things of improvement in the near future), things can now be televised and seen in all parts of the world as they happen.

When these Two Witnesses are killed and their bodies viewed for three and one-half days, the whole world (including apostate Israel) shall rejoice, leading to the giving of presents to one another. Truly, it will be a world-wide holiday!

After three and one-half days God raises them from the dead and takes them on up into heaven. In that same hour many are slain by an earthquake.

III. *The Trumpet Seven* (Read verses 15-19).

This Seventh Trumpet is sounded in the middle of the Tribulation **to announce judgment** upon the world. The Last Trump of I Corinthians 15 is not to be confused with the Seventh Trumpet. The Last Trump is the "forward march" order of God for the Church. This is sounded at the beginning of the Tribulation for the purpose of **taking the Church out** of this world. Another Trumpet shall be sounded **after** the Tribulation for the purpose (Matthew 24:29-31) of **gathering Israel** back to the Land.

At the sounding of this Seventh Trumpet we see that it not only covers the time of the first three and one-half years of the Tribulation, but that it is like another larger wave of the ocean which carries on beyond, even until the Coming of the Messiah (Christ) after the Tribulation. These words describe fully the fears of those who are without Christ as they realize that He has appeared.

The Book of Revelation
Chapter XII

Chapter 12 marks the beginning of the last half of the 70th Week of Daniel. These last three and one-half years of the Tribulation begin with the Anti-Messiah (Antichrist) breaking his covenant with Israel in the middle of the prophetic Week (see Daniel 9). The Nation Israel has fared sumptuously for the first three and one-half years, but now begins the Abomination of Desolation; truly, Jacob's trouble.

I. *The Woman* (Read verses 1, 2).

While the following Chapters (12-19) have to do with the last three and one-half years of the Tribulation, prophetically, they also give to us some historical events in the life of the Nation of Israel.

Israel is the woman arrayed in such fashion. It is she who was given the blessed privilege to bring forth into the world the Manchild — the Messiah. Of course, this event happened some 1900 years ago.

II. *The Dragon* (Read verses 3, 4).

The Dragon is none other than Satan, the Devil. He is revealed as having seven heads and ten horns; truly, he is organized with the angels who have followed him (the number is one-third), as declared in Ephesians 6:12.

The Dragon (Satan), with the Beast of Chapter 13 (he, too, having seven heads and ten horns — the Anti-Messiah), and the Beast that arises out of the earth (the False Prophet), compose the **UNHOLY TRINITY!** These three will be the **gods** of the **ungodly** during the Tribulation.

III. *The Child* (Read verses 5, 6).

The Child is the Virgin-born Messiah. How hard Satan tried to destroy Him upon His birth. Of course, being God manifested in the flesh, it was impossible for Satan to have killed Him.

As we consider these two verses we must note that a great time elapses between them. The Manchild, the Messiah, after His resurrection ascends unto Heaven to sit upon His Heavenly Father's throne. The time which elapses is the Church age. The sixth verse speaks of the time after the Church is raptured and the first three and one-half years of the Tribulation are over. This verse depicts the persecution of the Woman (Israel) and the deliverance of God for those who will not take the mark of the Beast (Antichrist). The place of security is said to be in the wilderness, and the time she is protected is one thousand, two hundred and sixty days, which is, of course, three and one-half years.

IV.   *The Archangel* (Read verses 7-12).

From these verses we learn of the coming battle in heaven, led by the Archangel, Michael, against Satan and his angels. Satan and his angels are cast out of the heavenlies, and with no other place to go, they are cast upon the earth. From time to time there has been the act of demonism, the act of men being possessed of devils; when Satan and his demons are cast here upon earth there shall be demon possession such as the world has never known.

When it shall be natural for men to be demon-possessed, it shall be supernatural to be God-possessed. There will be those who will overcome Satan and his demons by the Blood of the Lamb and by the word of their testimony. Certainly we can defeat him by these two weapons now!

V.   *The Nation* (Read verses 13-17).

Here again the Woman is mentioned — Israel — her persecutor and her deliverance. The place of refuge will be so located that sympathizing nations shall in some way supply this believing Jewish remnant with food, etc. Satan shall try to overthrow her with an army likened unto a flood, but natural causes are used by God to destroy her would-be executioners.

When this act of Satan is defeated he strives to destroy the people of Israel and all other believers who dwell outside of Palestine.

The Book of Revelation
Chapter XIII

"Like father, like son" is a familiar saying; this can be truthfully said of Satan and the Anti-Messiah (Antichrist). This chapter gives us a full description of the Man of Sin who shall be well organized here upon this earth during the Tribulation.

I. *The Beast of the Sea* (Read verses 1-9).

This beast does not only portray the Anti-Messiah, but it also portrays the kingdom over which he rules. The Beast has seven heads, showing to us that this empire shall have seven kings (see Chapter 17). One of these heads suffers a death stroke — this seventh head is the Anti-Messiah. Someone may ask, "How can the whole Beast be the Anti-Messiah and the Empire at the same time?" It is the same as when Hitler came to power; the cry in Germany was, "Hitler is Germany, and Germany is Hitler!" At the time of this Beast the cry shall be, "The Seventh Head is the World-Empire, and the World-Empire is the Seventh Head!"

The Seventh Head, although it suffers a death stroke, shall have a resurrection — truly, a mock Christ. Satan's messiah shall be raised from the dead by Satan, after being killed by a sword.

He is given the throne of Satan and Satan's power. No one seems to have power to make war with him. Also, power is given to this Head to make war with the saints of God. What persecution Satan shall carry on through this Anti-Messiah!

II. *The Beast Of The Earth* (Read verses 10-18).

This Beast exercises the same power as the first Beast. His duties are to cause the world to worship the first Beast (the Anti-Messiah) and to make an image unto him.

He gives power to the image that it may speak. In our modern day of science this has been accomplished over and over; that is, making images speak, etc. There is the modern day movie; then there is the robot, the mechanical man. Name it and it doesn't seem strange to us.

The second Beast carries out the mandate that no one can buy or sell, legally, without the mark, the name, or the number of the first Beast. We can understand fully the need of having a one-man rule by which the world can be fed properly, or proportionately, seeing there are so many crop failures during the Tribulation, etc., but to have the mandate of the world's food supply fall into the hands of the Anti-Messiah shall be fatal.

God tells us the number of the Beast; it is the number of a man, which is six (see Daniel 3). The Anti-Messiah's number is three sixes — 666! God is trying to tell us three times that the Beast, although performing many miracles, and although he is raised from the dead, is a man, is a Man, is a MAN!

The Book of Revelation
Chapter XIV

This is another parenthetical chapter, closely related to Chapter 7.

I. *The Servants on Earth* (Read verses 1-5).

These are the 144,000 Jewish ministers, servants or evangelists, or whatever one may want to call them; but we believe they are those who are sealed to preach during the last half of the Tribulation.

Their song is the glorifying of the Lord Jesus Christ. They are described as being virgins. It was the Lord Jesus who said when He was here nearly two thousand years ago, "For there are some eunuchs, which were so born from their mother's womb: and there are some eunuchs, which were made eunuchs of men: and there be eunuchs, which have made themselves eunuchs for the kingdom of heaven's sake" (Matthew 19:12). Truly, these 144,000 are these eunuchs declared by Christ Jesus. Their message is the Gospel of the Kingdom; hence, they do not marry, for the Kingdom of Heaven's sake. They cover the world without hindrance of wife or family, to preach the coming Kingdom of Heaven. But oh, what rewards shall be theirs!

II. *The Servant In Heaven* (Read verses 6, 7).

This servant is an angel. A better word for "preach" is **"announce."** God does not use heavenly beings to proclaim the Gospel of Christ in any age. This angel does **announce,** however, the beginning of the preaching of the Everlasting Gospel.

There are several adjectives which describe the Gospel. The Gospel, however, is the same: the death, burial and resurrection of Christ for the sins of mankind (I Corinthians 15:1-4). Today we are preaching the Gospel of the Grace of God — the same Gospel, with the emphasis upon **Grace;** the Gospel of the Kingdom which shall be preached by the

144,000 Jewish evangelists during the last half of the Tribulation is the same Gospel, but with the **Kingdom** emphasis. Whatever it be, the Gospel of the Grace of God, or the Gospel of the Kingdom, it is the same Gospel, and it is Eternal!

III. *The Servants of Satan* (Read verses 8-20).

Doom is pronounced upon those who take the mark of the Beast and who worship him.

Babylon is mentioned by name here, and on to the first part of Chapter 19 the nation of Babylon is set before us to be considered. It is true that Babylon has been prophesied to be destroyed and never rebuilt, but there are several things which have been spoken about Babylon which have not as yet been fulfilled. Consequently, Babylon shall be rebuilt; then these things which have been spoken about her shall be fulfilled, and she shall be destroyed and never seen again.

Babylon was never destroyed by the Medes and Persians. Even Alexander the Great died in Nebuchadnezzar's palace. The City of Babylon was existing even to the time of Christ, and John wrote one of his epistles from it.

Here in Chapter 14, verse 8, we see the fulfillment of Isaiah's prophecy, occurring at this time rather than in the past. Two chapters of Isaiah must yet be fulfilled concerning this city — 13 and 14.

Yes, the Scriptures tell us that Babylon shall become like Sodom, and we will never know where it was located. See Jeremiah 50 for other prophecies against Babylon. We know today where Babylon was, but one day it shall be destroyed and no one will ever know where it was located.

We believe in the revival of the Roman Empire (see Daniel 2 and 7), and we believe that she shall exist with the head (Anti-Messiah), who governs the world by his ten kings (see Chapter 17); we also believe that the headquarters shall be in the rebuilt city of Babylon. For your own enlightenment, turn to your present day encyclopedia and read up on the city of Hillah, which is located within the city limits of the old city of Babylon. It is a large city today.

Much persecution is brought about by the Anti-Messiah, and those who are killed by him for their refusal to worship false gods are indeed blessed of the Lord.

A wave of truth carries us unto the Battle of Armageddon in this chapter; it occurs at the end of the Tribulation.

Christ is He who shall tread out the winepress (see Chapter 19) in great, great judgment.

The Book of Revelation
Chapter XV

This chapter presents a vision in heaven. Chapter 16 states what happens on earth at the same time. There is rejoicing in heaven, but there is much suffering upon earth.

I. *The Servants* (Read verses 1, 2).

What a glorious group this is! These are they who are saved during the last half of the Tribulation and are slain for their faith. These are they who overcame the Beast by the Blood of the Lamb and by the word of their testimony (Chapter 12).

II. *Their Songs* (Read verses 3-8).

There are two songs they sing: The Song of Moses and The Song of the Lamb. The Song of the Lamb is found in this chapter, while the Song of Moses is found in Exodus 15.

Moses and the children of Israel had experiences like these who are delivered from the Anti-Messiah (Antichrist). Israel was delivered from Egypt; the Tribulation saints shall be delivered from sin. Israel was delivered from king Pharaoh, while the Tribulation saints shall be delivered from king Anti-Messiah. Israel sang her song of deliverance; the Tribulation saints shall sing their song of deliverance. Israel was saved to go into the wilderness; the Tribulation saints shall be saved to go into the Millennium. Only two from Israel went into the Promised Land; all Tribulation saints shall go into the Promised Land.

The Song of the Lamb is filled with praise unto the Lord Jesus Christ! Divine prediction is made that all nations (Gentiles) of the world shall worship Him; not only the nations (Gentiles) that shall exist at His coming, but every tongue of all ages shall worship Him — things in heaven, things on earth, and things under the earth. **All** men, past, present and future, shall confess that Jesus is Lord (Philippians 2:11).

With this Hallelujah chorus preparations are made in heaven for the last seven plagues to be visited upon the earth. God is **glorified,** not only in the praise of men, but also in the judgment upon sinful men. The Temple in Heaven is filled with the glory of God, as was the Tabernacle at the time of Moses, and as the Temple was in the time of Solomon.

The Book of Revelation

Chapter XVI

Chapter 16 completes the vision of Chapter 15. This takes place on earth. The seven angels are now commissioned to pour out their vials (bowls) of wrath upon the earth.

I. *First Vial* (Read verses 1, 2).

Truly, this judgment is of God. Only upon those who have taken the mark of the Beast shall this plague of sores fall.

II. *Second Vial* (Read verse 3).

We believe that the **Sea** is the Mediterranean Sea and not the people of the earth; if this be not the case, then every one will die during the Tribulation. This cannot be, for there are those who come out of the Tribulation alive, both saved and lost (Matthew 25:31-46).

Therefore, we hold that the souls mean all the living creatures of this Sea. What a blight upon the coastal cities, etc. With the death of all living creatures of the Sea, every kind of disease will prevail.

III. *Third Vial* (Read verses 4-7).

Fountains of pure water are polluted; they are turned into blood. Remember, back in Chapter 6 there are those whose souls are under the altar, who were slain during the first three and one-half years of the Tribulation for their faith; and they cried unto the Lord to avenge them? Here God does avenge them. Their executioners did shed their blood; therefore, God has given them blood to drink.

IV. *Fourth Vial* (Read verses 8, 9).

Because of the lack of water, drought and the scorching of the sun follows, but men shall blaspheme God all the more.

V. *Fifth Vial* (Read verses 10, 11).

Again we point out that you should take everything in the Book of Revelation as literally as possible.

This plague, similar to the one in Egypt, is of complete darkness, showing God's disapproval of the Beast and his kingdom. Still men blaspheme God, proving that judgment does not make believers out of unbelievers.

VI. *Sixth Vial* (Read verses 12-16).

This is the announcement of the coming of the Anti-Messiah's army from the East. A better translation for the word "east" is "land of the rising of the sun." In Chapter 9 we noted that this army shall consist of 200,000,000 (two hundred million) men. Where could this number be enlisted but from the nations of the Far East? The dictator of China has recently said that he could put an army of one hundred million men on the field in one day. Certainly the rest of the Far East could make up the remainder.

We believe that this great army shall fight with the Anti-Messiah (Antichrist) against the Lord Jesus Christ at Armageddon at the close of the Tribulation (see Chapter 19).

Verses 13 through 16 are parenthetical, revealing the fact that the rule and reign of the Anti-Messiah and the battle of Armageddon are Satan-inspired. All kings (dictators) shall be demon-possessed as they go out to battle Jehovah's Christ.

VII. *Seventh Vial* (Read verses 17-21).

With the pouring of this vial of wrath geographic changes are introduced. The elements of the earth and sky are employed to bring about this great judgment. Mountains fall back from whence they arose (this very thing has happened during our life time in the Far East); hail stones, 80 to 100 pounds in weight, shall fall; this truth is readily accepted when we learn that atomic explosions in the sea caused ice to fall in chunks of a ton or so in weight. Man has done it; can we doubt God?

Babylon comes to the forefront again. God Almighty is not through with that nation (City) as yet. It was several hundred years before the Messiah (Jesus Christ) came that the Babylonians took the Jewish people into exile on the direction of God, of course. They exercised too much persecution upon Israel, however, and God has not forgotten how they treated His people. "I will curse him that curseth thee" is being brought to its fullest during the Tribulation against Babylon.

The Book of Revelation
Chapter XVII

This chapter, along with Chapter 13, describes the rise, rule and ruin of the One World Religion and the One World Government. We trust that this study shall be a blessing to our readers as we endeavor to bring to you things which we have known for some time, which might prove to be new to you.

I. *The Scarlet Woman* (Read verses 1-7).

This woman depicts the One World Religion of the first three and one-half years of the Tribulation. This One World Religion is not just the unification of apostate Christianity, but it is the combination of the world's other religions, with the exception of Judaism. The Anti-Messiah has confirmed a covenant with the Jewish people at the beginning of the Tribulation, granting them liberty to worship in the new temple; thus, the Jewish people are free from uniting with the other religions of the world.

Some declare that this woman is the Religion of Rome. No doubt but that that religion will be included, but not to the exclusion of all of the other religions of the world.

She sits upon the Beast. Any creature is directed by its head, and every creature's head is guided by its rider. So it is in this case. The Beast is the One World Government, ridden by this harlot, who guides and directs its every move. We are not in doubt as to who she is, for her name is written upon her forehead: "BABYLON THE GREAT." Again there are those who say she is the Roman Religion, that the Roman Religion has idols, etc., and that that is the meaning of "harlotry." Harlotry is correctly interpreted to mean idol worship, but the Roman Religion is **not** the MOTHER of idolatry (she may be a daughter). BABYLON is the **mother** of idolatry! It was at Babylon and its tower where idolatry began, and all idolatry has stemmed from there. The worship of the woman and the child did not begin with the Roman Religion, but it began with the worship of Nimrod and his mother at Babylon and has existed since by other names in other religions of other countries.

This woman has been made drunk with the blood of saints (Old Testament saints) and with the blood of the martyrs of Jesus (New Testament saints). In every age she has existed since Babylon. She shall raise her whorish head in defiance of things pure and good in the Lord Jesus Christ and shall cause the world to embrace her.

II. *The Scarlet Beast* (Read verses 8-18).

We have already learned (see Chapter 13) that this Beast shall be the revived Fourth Empire and that its seventh head, which suffers a death stroke (dies) and is healed (resurrected), is the Anti-Messiah (Antichrist).

We would like to point out something new here concerning the seven mountains. At once we are prone to say that they are the seven hills of Rome. But why could they not be the seven hills of some other city as well? But now when we see the value of one little word in the 10th verse the whole description takes on a different meaning. "And **there** are seven kings." The word **"there"** is better rendered **"they"** — "and **they** are seven kings." Let us turn to verse 9 and read on through verse 10; we have now a much better translation: "And here is the mind which hath wisdom. The seven heads are seven mountains, on which the woman sitteth. And **these** are seven kings: five are fallen, and one is, and the other is not yet come; and when he cometh, he must continue a short space. And the beast that was, and is not, even he is the eighth, and is of the seven, and goeth into perdition." In other words, the seven heads are seven mountains, and these are seven kings; — 7 heads equal 7 mountains, which equal 7 kings.

We know that during the first half of the Tribulation the world government shall be ruled by seven kings. The last king shall suffer death by a sword and then be raised from the dead. He shall be considered, not only as the seventh head, but as the eighth also. His death and resurrection take place in the middle of the 70th Week of Daniel (Tribulation); no wonder the world worships him! No wonder he places his throne in the Temple at Jerusalem and declares himself to be God.

Two great things take place immediately. He is now completely sovereign. He is HEAD of the One World Government. Now he is to be the POTENTATE of the One World Religion!

He places his throne in the Temple, declares himself to be God, and then destroys the Temple and the city of Jerusalem. The religion of Judaism is destroyed! The Beast's (Anti-Messiah's) ten kings, who have given their power to him, destroy the Harlot (Babylon) at this time. The Beast is now supreme; he alone is to be worshipped! For three and one-half years he rules and is worshipped.

These ten kings who rule the world for the Beast will fight with him against the Lord Jesus Christ at the Battle of Armageddon.

Again the woman is declared to be the City of Babylon; in this case she is the World's capital, both commercially and religiously. Her destruction occurs in the **middle** of the Tribulation.

The Book of Revelation
Chapter XVIII

As we continue with this study of the destruction of Babylon, we would point out that we believe that it is a literal city and the capital of the Revived Fourth World Government. If this were not so, why didn't the sacred writer, by inspiration of the Holy Spirit, spell the name ROME out in these many chapters? Babylon, as prophesied in the Old Testament Scriptures, is herein quoted as being destroyed at this time. This destruction occurs in the middle of the Tribulation.

I. *Its Doom Commanded* (Read verses 1-8).

More of the Old Testament Scriptures are quoted here, announcing the doom of the world's capital. Judgment is thrust upon her for her persecution of God's earthly people, the Jews. Someone may ask, "Why? That happened 2500 years ago!" But God hasn't forgotten. He is proving to us how sincere His Word is. One cannot touch His own, or His anointed, without His wrath being showered upon him.

Here in this city there are those who have not worshipped the Woman, and God calls His believers out before destruction comes. It was the same at the time of the flood; Noah and his family were called out. At the time of Sodom, Lot and his family were allowed to escape. And at the time of the coming Tribulation God shall call the Church home before it begins.

II. *Its Doom Consummated* (Read verses 9-19).

The very words of this Scripture passage fully portray the annihilation of this great city. Men here in Babylon, as at Ephesus at the time of Paul, were made rich with the things sold to the worshippers of idols, etc. In one short hour the city was leveled. This also reminds one of the city of Jerusalem's destruction by Titus in 70 A.D. Forty years before its fall the Lord Jesus had foretold it. When Titus surrounded the city he gave the people the opportunity to escape if they would. The only ones whose lives were spared were the Christians. Here in Babylon the only people to be delivered from the destruction of this great city will be the believers who heed God's call to flee.

III. *The Doom Completed* (Read verses 20-24).

God is always glorified in all things, even as far as the fall of His enemies is concerned. One day it will be impossible to find a trace of Babylon. Heaven rejoices over this judgment.

This seems strange, but yet it is not; God does use the Anti-Messiah (Antichrist) to destroy this Babylon — (the One World Religion); and then His Son, Jesus Christ, shall destroy the Anti-Messiah! Yes, God uses many times those who were against Him to chastise other of His enemies.

The Book of Revelation
Chapter XIX

The first six verses of this chapter are a continuation of the judgment of the harlot, Babylon. Babylon rules as the One World Religion for the first three and one-half years of the Tribulation. In the middle of the Tribulation Babylon is destroyed by the Beast, the Anti-Messiah. This chapter now takes up with the destruction of the Anti-Messiah (Antichrist).

I. *Rejoicing in Heaven* (Read verses 1-6).

More and more praise is made unto God, because He has judged this one who not only caused the death of many believers during the first three and one-half years of the Tribulation, but who also caused the death of many who were saved in past ages.

II. *Release of the Bride* (Read verses 7-10).

By "release" we mean the Bride becoming the **Wife!** As customs of the East provide, the Bride is espoused to the husband first; then a period elapses before the two may live together. So it is with the Church (the Bride); we have been espoused to the Lord Jesus (2 Corinthians 11:2), and the waiting period has already lasted nearly 2,000 years! However, it will not be long until we shall be and ever live with the Lord!

Her array is the white linen of the righteousnesses of the saints. This is better rendered, "righteous acts of the saints." Oh, may we adorn ourselves with works of righteousness!

Those who are invited are indeed blessed! These who are invited cannot be the saints of the Church, for the Church is the Bride. We believe the invited guests are the Old Testament saints and the Tribulation saints who have been martyred but are now resurrected.

We hold that the marriage supper of the Lamb occurs just

at the end of the Tribulation (in heaven) just before the Lord returns with His saints.

III. *Return of Christ* (Read verses 11-21).

The Second Coming of Christ is clearly taught in the Old Testament. Many of the Jewish people have confused the first coming with the second coming. It is hard for them to see the first coming of the Messiah in rejection, but it is there, right in the Word of God! Israel today awaits the coming of the Messiah in glory and power, including the judging of the world in righteousness and the putting down of His enemies forever.

And we Christians look for the coming of the Messiah in the same light, only we believe that the **first** coming that the Jewish people await of their Messiah is in truth the **Second** Coming of our Christ.

We Christians believe the Old Testament Scriptures when they point out the rejection of the Messiah during His first coming, and we look forward to the fulfillment of the Old Testament Scriptures where they speak of His second coming in **power.**

When He returns, we shall come with Him! Hallelujah! His armies of heaven follow Him. Soon He is to be in Battle array; soon He is to destroy His enemies; soon He is to tread the winepress of the fierceness and wrath of Almighty God in judgment!

The battle is Armageddon. The army of 200 million (see Chapters 9 and 16) fights, but it is of no avail. **All** men, except the Beast (Anti-Messiah) and his False Prophet, are killed. All of the true Messiah's enemies have been subdued. The Anti-Messiah and his False Prophet are then cast into the Lake of Fire.

The Book of Revelation
Chapter XX

The events of this chapter closely follow those of Chapter 19.

I. *Satan* (Read verses 1-3).

Satan (the Devil), that old Dragon, the Serpent who beguiled Eve, is taken and bound with chains and cast into the very, very deep abyss — the bottomless pit. The time is for 1,000 years. The Scriptures here state that he shall be loosed for a short season after the 1,000 years are over. We know what he will do during this time when he is loosed, but as to the reason why, we leave that to the omniscience of God.

II. *Saints* (Read verses 4-6).

Do you remember the saints who were killed during the first three and one-half years of the Tribulation (see Chapter 6) and their request for vengeance? Remember, also, they were told to rest just a while longer until their brethren and fellow servants would be killed as they had been? Here in this portion are those who are slain during the last three and one-half years of the Tribulation.

The very time of their testimony and faith is fully stated; they would not take the mark of the Beast, etc. This could not happen until the Beast (Anti-Messiah) sets himself up as God in the midst of the Tribulation. Yes, they are slain for their faith; they live and reign with the Lord Jesus; they are raised from the dead just after the Tribulation is over — the same as with the Old Testament saints (see Daniel 12).

The rest of the dead, the lost from Adam to the last sinner who dies in the Millennium, are not raised until the 1,000 years are over.

These who were slain for their faith complete the FIRST RESURRECTION. The FIRST RESURRECTION is composed of four parts: (1) the Lord Jesus Christ; (2) The Church; (3) The Two Witnesses; (4) The Old Testament and Tribulation Saints (see Daniel 12).

III. *Sinners* (Read verses 7-14).

These are sinners who are living at the close of the Millennium, when Satan is loosed for a season; they follow him to try to overthrow the Kingdom of the Lord Jesus Christ. Where did these sinners come from? They are the children born of saved parents, who came out of the Tribulation alive.

It is true that no sinners (unbelievers) will be permitted to enter the Kingdom (1,000 year reign of Christ). We, the Church, shall reign with the Messiah in our glorified bodies; yet, there shall be those who are saved who come out of the Tribulation alive, whose bodies are not changed and who will be permitted to continue to have children. When these saints get their glorified bodies we do not know.

The children who are born during the Millennium will have to be born again the same as their parents. We are told in Isaiah 65:20 that there shall be death during this time, but it is the death of sinners only, and that is when the sinner reaches the age of 100.

During the Millennium, with Christ reigning, the people born at this time will be given the privilege of worshipping the Messiah. Should they reach the age of 100 and fail to accept Him, they shall be accursed and shall die.

At the close of the Millennium, when Satan is loosed, there shall be countless numbers (as the sand of the sea) of those 99 years and younger who have not been saved who will follow Satan against the Messiah. Fire from heaven falls and destroys them.

Satan is then cast into the Lake of Fire prepared for him and his angels.

Immediately following, the wicked dead (of all ages) are raised from the dead to stand before the Great White Throne. You will rejoice to notice that **NO** saint stands before this judgment throne — only **sinners!**

Several Books (Scrolls) are opened to judge the sinners. The Book of Life is a Witness against them; their names are not recorded therein. I do not doubt but that the Word of

God is another Witness against them, for the Lord Jesus said that His Words (the Word of God) should judge the lost in that day. And last of all, the Book which records their works shall judge them. Yes, even as the saint shall be rewarded according to his works, so shall the sinner be judged according to his works. As there are degrees of rewards, so also shall there be degrees of punishment.

Everything that has held the souls of the damned shall give up its charges. Hades (translated here as 'hell') shall give up the dead; this is the place of the damned after death; death shall give up its dead (the condition or state of these wicked).

Then all are cast into the Lake of Fire. We believe this to be a literal place. It is called the **Second Death**. The **Second Death** is not utter destruction. Death in Scripture always means "separation." The first death (physical) is the separation of the soul and spirit from the body; the **second death** is the eternal separation of the damned from the presence of God.

Who are sent there? Those whose names are not recorded in the Book of Life!

The Book of Revelation
Chapter XXI

Chronologically the events of this chapter follow immediately the happenings of Chapter 20.

At the raising of the wicked dead the first heaven and earth flee away. Since the wicked have been judged, a new heaven and a new earth appear, either renewed or re-created.

I. *The Parade of Things New* (Read verses 1-7).

We know from the Scriptures that there are three heavens: (1) the immediate space above us; (2) the space of the stars; and (3) the space, or place, of the abode of God. Hence, we call your attention to the fact that it is the **first heaven** that is cleared, renewed and purified. If we would only stop for a moment and see how man today is polluting the space above us, we would see readily why there shall be a need to renew it, The earth shall also need renovation, although it has brought forth good things for 1,000 years. It needs to be purified, too.

Look at the redeemed people. What joy shall be theirs forever! Nothing of this past life with its pain, heartaches and death shall ever be known again.

The Blessed Messiah guarantees heirship and sonship to all who are overcomers — those who believe that Jesus is the Son of God (I John 5:4,5).

II. *The Predicament of People Lost* (Read verse 8).

This verse clarifies the plight of those not saved. Their doom is the Lake of Fire, although it was not prepared for them; it was prepared for Satan and his angels. Yet, the unbelievers (the lost) shall go there.

Look at those who are classified as going to hell. We need no one to help us interpret their sins, but we would like to point to the **"fearful** and the **unbelieving."** The fearful are cowards, those who would not stand and believe in the Lord Jesus Christ. The unbelieving can be classed in these three divisions: (1) those who plainly refused to believe in the Messiah; (2) those who were going to, but failed in time to make their profession; and (3) those who had good intentions, but were **misled**. These are the most pathetic of all. Someone did not tell them correctly that they had only to believe that Christ died for their sins, and that He was buried, and that He rose again from the dead bodily.

III. *The Presentation of the Bride's City* (Read verses 9-21).

Any city can be thought of in two ways: (1) the people; and (2) the place where the people live. The Bride can be thought of in the same two ways: (1) Those who were saved during the Dispensation of Grace; and (2) the Place, the City out of Heaven, where she is to live with her Lord.

The city is **not** heaven; it is a city that comes out of Heaven. From the description it is about 1400 square miles. How beautiful this city must be. Those who have lived in its suburbs (in a dying condition) have testified of her spires and beautiful buildings!

The foundations are twelve, named for the twelve apostles, with twelve gates of pearl named for the twelve tribes of Israel. **Shame on those who do not love the people of Israel!** God shows us that the very entrances to this city have been named for the twelve tribes! Yes, we would like to repeat this over and over again. By naming the gates thusly, God shows us Gentiles that truly the entrance into the Gospel, hence into the City of Heaven itself, has come by means of the Jewish people.

The streets are pure gold; I believe it to be as the Word says. This is good enough for all of us.

IV. *The Place of Eternity's Worship* (Read verse 22).

The Temple is God Almighty, Who is the Lamb. As God dwelt among His people in the Tabernacle, and later in the Temple, so shall He dwell among His people by means of His Son.

V. *The Power of Heaven's Light* (Read verses 23-27).

There will be no need of the sun, nor of the moon; and

there will be no need of man's artificial light. The Lamb is the Light. True, He is our Light and there is no darkness in Him at all, even in this life; but in the Life to come, He will be the actual Light of all heaven and for all of His people. And there shall be no night there — no darkness of any kind prevails; there will be no sin, no sinners — nothing of darkness.

Only the saved, those whose names are written in the Lamb's Book of Life, will dwell there.

The Book of Revelation
Chapter XXII

This chapter continues to describe things as they shall be after the Millennium and the Great White Throne.

Sometimes it seems that we are in Eternity as we study this great chapter, and at other times it seems we are back in the Millennium, as the same situation seemingly is declared in Isaiah 65 and 66. It is true that during the 1,000 year reign of Messiah (Christ) there shall be a river with all manner of fruit for all people. It is a picture of that great River of Life in Heaven which shall be for the enjoyment of all the saints in glory.

I. *The Last Prophecy* (Read verses 1-16).

Living Waters shall be for those who are born again. One might say that all these things are merely symbolic, but we love to think of them as being real for the children of God.

The condition of mankind is forever set when death occurs, and these Scriptures prove it. If man is filthy and unrighteous, and dies that way, he will remain that way forever; nothing throughout eternity will change the mind of God to relieve his suffering or give him another chance to be saved. But praise the Lord, those who are righteous will never lose that position! Nothing will ever be able to change our salvation — simply nothing! We shall be righteous still — the children of God forever!

When the Lord returns He shall bring His rewards with Him: (1) He rewards His Bride at the Rapture, **before** the Tribulation (1 Corinthians 1:7,8; 3:11-15); and (2) He rewards the Old Testament and Tribulation saints **after** the Tribulation (Daniel 12:2; Revelation 11:18).

II. *The Last Invitation* (Read verse 17).

It is the Lord's nature to save. He died to save sinful man 2,000 years ago. Today, by the Holy Spirit and the Bride (the Church), He extends His glorious invitation to come and drink of the water of life — SALVATION — which He alone provides. The call is to **you** should you be without Christ. Won't **you** trust Him as your Lord and Saviour today?

III. *The Last Warning* (Read verses 18 and 19).

Sinners, beware if you should try to alter the words of this Book. Add to it, and the plagues shall be added to you; subtract words from it, and your name shall be taken away from the Book of Life (better rendered "Trees of Life"). No, we shall not add to it, nor take away from it, for we believe it to be God's Word and have trusted the Christ it has offered.

IV. *The Last Prayer* (Read verses 20 and 21).

The Lord declares He shall come; His coming for us shall be the time when the "things that are" — the Church age — is over. Our prayers in this day of the ending of the Dispensation of Grace should be, "Come, Lord Jesus!"

Oh, may the Bride of Christ today begin to earnestly pray that prayer!

Roy F. Brown